MISFIT CHEF

MISFIT CHEF

STORIES & RECIPES FROM MEMORY

CHRISTOPHER J. DESTEFANO
WITH PHOTOGRAPHY BY CYNTHIA AUGUST

TABLETOP
PUBLICATIONS

Copyright © 2024 by Christopher J. DeStefano

All rights reserved.

No part of this book may be reproduced, or stored in a retrieval system, or transmitted in any form or by any means, electronic, mechanical, photocopying, recording, or otherwise, without express written permission of the publisher.

Some names and identifying details have been changed to protect the privacy of individuals.

Published by Tabletop Publications, Ipswich, MA
www.misfitchefcookbook.com

GIRL FRIDAY PRODUCTIONS

Edited and designed by Girl Friday Productions
www.girlfridayproductions.com

Design: Rachel Marek
Project management: Kristin Duran
Editorial production: Abi Pollokoff
Photography: Cynthia August
Image credits: All cover and interior photography by Cynthia August, except as noted. Photos on pages xiv, xv, xvi, xxi, 31 (Christopher at counter), 41, 133, 135, 152, 153, 158, and 162 were provided by the author. Photo on spine © sumire8/Shutterstock, pages ii–iii © mexrix/Shutterstock, pages 32–33 © Brett Taylor Photography/Shutterstock, cutlery icons throughout © kristinasavkov/Shutterstock.

ISBN (hardcover): 979-8-9903613-0-0
ISBN (ebook): 979-8-9903613-1-7
Library of Congress Control Number: 2024906852

First edition

To my grandparents, for showing me the
power of food and the good in people

I would like to express my heartfelt gratitude to everyone who contributed to the creation and publication of this book. It is through their collective effort, support, and inspiration that this project has come to fruition.

THANK YOU

BOB
for being the rock upon which our family sits, I love you

MOM AND DAD
for raising me to be the man that I am today

CYNTHIA AUGUST
for your willingness to always jump in and come along on all of my crazy rides

DOUG BRENDEL
for hearing my voice and helping me find it

MARGO MALONEY
for believing every step of the way, even when I didn't

BILL RHOADES
for donating crucial transcription services

JOAN REES
"for everything I am and ever will be"

CONTENTS

Author's Note — ix

Introduction — xi
   Without Pirates, and No Tattoos — xi

I. Setting the Table — 1
Into the Abyss — 2
- Coconut Cupcakes with Cream Cheese Frosting — 15
- Christopher's Chocolate Cake — 16
- Perfect Chicken Salad — 19
- Oven-Fried Chicken — 20
- Jam Thumbprint Cookies — 23
- Christopher's Marinated Steak Tips — 24
- Classic Whoopie Pies — 27
- Classic Marshmallow Filling — 28

II. See What Sticks — 33
Here, Let Me Show You — 34
- Roast Pork Tenderloin with Poached Plums — 47
- Warm Arugula Salad with Caramelized Red Onion, Pancetta, and Pine Nuts — 48
- Orecchiette with Sausage and Broccolini — 51
- Tom's Date-Night Seared Salmon with Maple-Soy Glaze — 52
- Crispy Polenta with Rosemary — 55
- Chocolate-Dipped Almond Biscotti — 56

III. Farm Fabulous — 61
No Kitchen, No Problem — 62
- Blackberry and Thyme Margarita — 73
- Farmhouse Gazpacho — 74
- Watermelon Salad with Feta — 77
- Roasted Vegetable Tart with Goat Cheese Custard — 78
- Grilled Flank Steak with Blistered Vegetables and Herbs — 81
- Grilled Peaches with Mascarpone Cream and Crumbled Amaretti — 82

IV. The Good Kid — 87
What Do You Want to Do? — 88
   Chicken Cordon Peter — 98

V. Fire and Friendship — 101
The Martha Stewart Moment — 102
   Herb Salad Spring Rolls — 111
   Spicy Peanut Sauce — 113
   Spicy Tuna Tartare on Wonton Crisps — 114
   Caramelized Onion Dip — 117
   Heirloom Tomato and Nectarine Salad with Whipped Feta — 118
   Grilled Squash Ribbons and Prosciutto with Mint Dressing — 121

VI. It's Complicated — 125
Vive la France! — 126
   French 75 Cocktail — 139
   Gougères—French Cheese Puffs — 140
   Quiche au Fromage — 143
   Moules Frites — 144
   Brussels Sprouts Lardons — 147
   French Strawberry Tart — 148
   Chocolate Pots de Crème — 151

VII. Corral the Queens — 155
Buy Someone a Drink — 156
   Spiced Fried Chickpeas — 169
   Roasted Red Pepper and Goat Cheese Arancini — 170
   Individual Chicken Potpies — 173
   Spicy Thai Steamed Mussels in Coconut Curry Broth — 177
   Red Wine-Braised Short Ribs with Creamy Polenta — 178
   Red Wine-Poached Pears with Mascarpone Filling — 181

VIII. Debauchery by Degrees — 185
Where's Daddy? — 186

About the Author — 197

AUTHOR'S NOTE

Some cookbooks take a traditional approach to presenting their recipes, often beginning with starter courses and ending with desserts. Some take a categorical approach, choosing to showcase recipes by season or region.

As a cookbook memoir, *Misfit Chef* offers each chapter as a distinct memory from Christopher's Table, which operated as a bakery, prepared-food shop, wine bar, and restaurant from 2008 to 2014. Each chapter explores and celebrates a unique culinary experience that occurred at the bar, in the kitchen, under a tent in a cornfield, or even in France. The recipes and stories are time and place specific to each chapter.

INTRODUCTION

Without Pirates, and No Tattoos

Whenever someone asked what I did for a living, the words got stuck in my throat.

I dreaded referring to myself as a chef, mostly because I didn't believe I was one. I certainly didn't feel like one.

Sure, I could cook. I had knife skills, and I even owned a crisp white chef's jacket. Yet something was missing.

I felt like an imposter.

Chefs were burly, gruff, decisive, and confident; they possessed stamina, pain tolerance, and grace under pressure. These were tattooed, foulmouthed pirates who played with sharp knives.

But that wasn't me. I was different.

As a kid, I grew up feeling different; throughout grade school and high school, I struggled with the idea of who I was, and it wasn't until college that I eventually came to grips with my sexuality as a gay man. So in a very real way—maturing in the food world, coming of age as a chef—the feeling was familiar to me. Similar to my struggles as a kid, I went through a culinary coming-out process as a chef. Feeling like an outsider, a misfit, I eventually came to terms with my culinary identity, and ultimately accepted and embraced who and what I was professionally.

Different.

In culinary terms, I understand that chefs find food sensual. I can appreciate its beauty. But at the end of the day, that's not what gives my meringue stiff peaks . . . because, for me, it's not about the food.

And no, that's not a typo.

It's not about the food *for me*.

It took me more than half my working career to understand this, but I'm finally here, and I stand by it.

Yes, in some ways, this makes me a culinary outlier—but I'm okay with that.

So here we are. Me writing and cooking, you reading and wondering, *What the hell?*

But before you write me off as a chef who doesn't believe he's a chef and who thinks cooking isn't about the food, please let me explain. I promise I will not only show you the power of food and how it helps bind us to the best bits of life, but also answer the question, If it's not about the food, then what *is* it about?

The beginning of the answer is simply this: for me, the food was never enough.

The idea of spending my entire career in the solitary confinement of the kitchen, cooking in a self-imposed exile, seasoning and plating each dish only to watch it be whisked away through the swinging door, never to be seen again—this was a hurdle I simply could not get over.

I wanted more.

I needed to follow the dish out of the kitchen and into the world beyond. It was crucial for me to witness the magical transformation that took place . . . not on the stove, but on the *table*, where the meal was *shared*. Food was the catalyst, the foreplay that stimulated conversation and brought people together. I needed to lose myself in the stories that the food helped evoke, and to see and know the people behind them.

For me, the food was never enough.

And when the final champagne cork popped with an explosion of laughter, I longed for a place at the table, among friends with full bellies and empty plates. Satiated. Contented in the afterglow.

How did I become this strange misfit who believed that the focus should be less on the food and more on the people? The answer can be found somewhere circa 1969. We all have a point of origin—not just the place where we were born but the place where we were *made*. And this is mine . . .

Just across the harbor from Boston's impressive skyline sat an enclave of neighborhoods. East Boston: where I learned to ride a bike and throw a ball, where I watched my grandmother make her Sunday gravy and learned to make it myself. East Boston—on the Blue Line, only one train stop away from Boston, but somehow far enough to be another planet.

Irish neighborhoods were everywhere in Boston, which left the Italians to settle in either the North End or through the tunnel and under the harbor to "Eastie." Eastie was its own version of Boston, but instead of brownstones and row houses, we had vinyl-sided three-decker walk-ups, each floor a family, and every street was packed with them. Sharing the city with Logan Airport, we grew accustomed to the smell of jet fuel and the deafening roar of airplanes, some flying so low, you thought they might just snag Mrs. DiLuigi's third-floor laundry line.

In the early mornings, Chubby's corner bakery would begin making little mounded Italian egg cookies, dipped in white icing and dashed with multicolored sprinkles. Sweet perfume—confectioners' sugar and vanilla—would waft out into the streets, gently overpowering the acrid *eau de jetliner* and nudging the sleepy neighborhood awake.

During summer days, the streets were our playground. Constant games of stickball or street hockey, pausing only for the occasional passing car. We knew all the shortcuts and getaways through the city blocks for evading cops or firefighters looking to screw down fire hydrants we'd busted open on a hot day. Like mini urban ninjas, we scaled fences to escape a furious Mary D'Angelis, screaming at us for letting our popsicles melt on her freshly swept and washed sidewalk. From East Eagle all the way down to Condor Street, across the whole vacant lot on Putnam, and up past the Sheridan school to the City Yards—Eastie was safe. Familiar. And it was ours.

After supper, on warm evenings, people gathered on their stoops, drinking iced coffee or homemade wine, and chatted with their neighbors, a singsong staccato of broken English peppered with Italian words and phrases.

And then, inevitably, the streetlights buzzed, flickered a few times, and finally snapped on to signal that dusk was approaching—a message to all us kids: time to go home.

It was a city of concrete bathtub Madonnas and iron fire escapes, in a time when neighborhood messages were delivered in person. It was a place where everyone knew one another and old ladies wearing sleeveless housecoats sat at their spotless windows, sentinels keeping an ever-watchful eye on the neighborhood.

In the heart of this world, at the corner of Prescott and Lexington, was a tiny grocery store, so tucked away, so completely blended into the backdrop of the neighborhood, if you didn't know it was there you might miss it—but everyone in East Boston knew it was there.

This tiny market, a street-level store with three apartments stacked above it, was the absolute center of my universe.

Two oversized storefront windows were divided by a central

Left: *My grandmother Millie behind the counter at my grandparents' butcher shop / grocery store in East Boston, MA;* Right: *My grandfather Libby at work behind his butcher block*

entrance. Walk into the store, take it all in, and any first impression could be reduced to a single word: *abundance*. The shelves were stocked floor to ceiling—but neatly and orderly, products always front facing. Wonderful, endless smells, fresh bread or fresh ground Italian sausage, hung in the air. The soundtrack: chatty customers speaking a part-English, part-Italian language, gathering ingredients for their passed-down family recipes. How to describe it all? A frenzy? A flurry? It was orderly chaos. There was a never-ceasing rhythm, and it danced the tarantella out into the neighborhood, with every order packaged up and carried out that central door, to become the occasion for family and friends to gather around a table, to eat and connect.

This market was owned and operated by my grandparents. They could always be found at their respective positions. My grandfather Liberato—always known as Libby, though I called him Papa—behind his massive butcher block. And my grandmother Carmella—only ever known as Millie, though I called her Nana—behind the cash register.

The floor-to-ceiling shelves, with everything the neighborhood needed—fresh bread, produce, dairy, dry goods—all of this, my

Left: *My aunt, Marie, and her husband, Bobby, taking grocery orders over the phone at my grandparents' butcher shop / grocery store in East Boston, MA;* Right: *My grandmother Millie stocking the shelves in the grocery store*

grandmother oversaw. My grandfather ran the other side of the store; the deli, butcher block, and meat case were under his watch.

It was the late 1970s and I wasn't even a decade old, but I had already become a fixture in my grandparents' shop. I was raised among the cardboard boxes, Table Talk Pies, and penny candy, surrounded by a dazzling cast of characters: customers, delivery people, and relatives all weaving in and out of the store and our lives with an easy familiarity.

My feet would dangle above the floor as I sat on an oversized radiator with my back to the storefront window, just to the right of my grandfather. I would watch him, study him with a childlike wonder and curiosity, matched only by my absolute adoration of him. He would work away behind his butcher block, filling the meat case, grinding hamburger, slicing deli meats. He was a burly mountain of a man, almost twice as wide as he was tall, with a barrel chest that rolled right down into his enormous belly. He was always draped in a white apron randomly dotted and stained with the results of an honest day's work. Wielding a meat cleaver, he was surely a formidable and impressive sight; yet to me, he was the most gentle and loving and safe human being I'd ever encountered. His giant hands,

Left: *My grandfather Libby with my cousin Allie*; Right: *My grandmother Millie and my aunt, Marie, waiting on customers at my grandparents' butcher shop / grocery store in East Boston, MA*

with sausage-like fingers, were equally adept at taking apart pork ribs and wiping away a little boy's tears.

On the other side of the store, my grandmother buzzed between the shelves, plucking cans of tomatoes, grabbing boxes of macaroni, packing them alongside fruit, vegetables, meat, and milk in cardboard delivery boxes. If my grandfather represented the "back of the house," then my grandmother was, without a doubt, the front. She would meet and greet customers as they entered the store, spend time with them, and help them find what they needed. She took orders over the telephone, stocked shelves, ran the cash register, and oversaw any money changing hands—she was perpetual motion.

Nana could barely see over the top of the cash register—standing on her spindly legs—but she was a force to be reckoned with, and I never saw her tired . . . ever. She kept a dozen plates spinning at any moment, and none of them ever suffered a crack. I was in awe of her.

> If my grandfather represented the "back of the house," then my grandmother was, without a doubt, the front.

One indelible little memory loop: I'm six years old, standing on a chair in my grandparents' apartment, "helping" my grandmother cook. The magic she makes, turning eggs and flour into pasta . . . breathing in the aroma of oil and garlic as it crashes into a heated pan, a whiff of her perfume . . . and the tidbits of food and wisdom she offers me, like delicious secrets that no one else will ever know—it's nirvana for a little boy.

What she created for our whole family in hand-me-down pots, pans, and Tupperware transcended the word *food*. Her magic was the thread that stitched our family tapestry together and held it strong.

As a chubby-cheeked little kid on the store's radiator, I soaked in the sights and sounds all around me. The clangy, muffled bell-strike ring of the rotary telephone cut through the store chatter again and again: someone in need of something, a neighbor, a connection. My grandmother, quick to snap up the receiver: "Hello, Millie's Market." Teenage boys from the neighborhood perked up when the phone rang. They worked as "order boys," loading boxes of groceries into the back of an old station wagon; my mother was their faithful driver.

With a steady stream of customers and deliveries rotating in and out of the small store throughout the day, my grandparents were constantly talking and working, working and talking. They fretted about late deliveries and the dairy case needing repair, debated a run to the bank to get more change for the cash register—but much more than that: they talked with their customers. Millie always had a pot of coffee brewing in the back room, and she offered a cup to anyone who passed through the door. With this simple act of hospitality, repeated authentically and ceaselessly, she gathered a sense of how everyone in the neighborhood was doing. Even as a little kid, I came to recognize my grandmother's loving look of concern. And when I heard her say to a customer, "Let's talk," the translation was always clear: something was going on in somebody's family. Millie and her customer would go into the back or off to the side of the store and talk, sometimes for hours.

It was another era—an era of small local markets, when grocery stores were the epicenters of their neighborhoods, places where you could come to know and understand the character of a community. Over time, as the markets got "super," they also got a lot less personal, lost their intimacy. Barber- and beauty shops became the places where locals gathered and chatted. But back in the 1970s and '80s, if you wanted to know what was going on in my neighborhood, you'd ask Libby and Millie. To me, it makes sense: barber- and beauty shops make you feel good from the outside in, but food makes you feel good from the inside out.

The small market of my childhood era was a community touchstone, a neighborhood gathering spot, a place where people could talk about issues of importance to them—local gossip, sports, politics, community affairs—while they shopped. And at the center of it all were my grandparents, running a business but also investing in people, in community. It was a time when sitting around the dinner table was a daily custom, and my grandparents knew what was on every family's table and in every family's pantry. They knew who needed a few extra cutlets after the meat came off the scale, or a loaf of bread my Nana "forgot" to ring up.

I would get confused when I saw customers fill up their grocery bags and depart without paying.

"Can I put it on the cuff?" they would ask.

I tried to wrap my kid brain around this strange concept as my grandmother removed a small black book from under the counter, flipped through its dog-eared pages, and made small notations. Years later, I came to understand that many of my grandparents' customers lived paycheck to paycheck and sometimes needed a little help. A regular customer who recently lost a job, another whose husband gambled his paycheck away at the dog track . . . Libby and Millie graciously extended credit, free from judgment—or even terms.

> The small market of my childhood era was a community touchstone, a neighborhood gathering spot.

Today, I wouldn't believe it had ever existed if I hadn't lived through it. Imagine a grocery store these days extending credit to customers, with no expectation of return on investment. Imagine a grocery store as a place to share a delicate family situation (with the owner as a trusted confidant) and find solutions for getting through it. Imagine, after a blizzard, my dad and my uncle pulling sleds laden with store deliveries because cars couldn't traverse roads not yet plowed.

But to my grandparents, all this was simply a matter of wanting to make sure their customers never had to go without.

It wasn't just a business. It was life.

It isn't just food. It's *people*.

You couldn't get more "mom and pop" than my grandparents' store. Our entire family lived above it. On one side, my great-grandparents. On the other side, my other great-grandparents. Above them, my grandparents. An aunt with a talking parrot. A boarder who paid rent.

But on the street level—in fact, four steps down from the sidewalk—was the store.

The store.

If there's ever a snapshot setting that best represents my childhood, this is it. And if heaven truly exists, then, God willing, my grandparents' tiny grocery store on Lexington Street is what will be waiting for me.

My grandfather's butcher block stood straight and sturdy throughout all the years of his work, and under all the conversations my grandparents had with every customer. Every hard time, every joy, every celebration. Even the eventual decision to close the store when my grandparents were able to retire. That butcher block still stands straight and sturdy today, in my own kitchen—a piece of living history. The surface was planed down many times over the years, to keep up with my grandfather's chopping, and it has been planed down many times since it was bequeathed to me. But it is the one thing from Millie's Market that has become my everything, the honest and pure truth that I have come to know. To me it's an altar—an altar upon which my grandparents made a daily sacrifice, putting their family and customers first so that they might know something better. This butcher block is a stage on which my grandparents performed acts of kindness and generosity. It represents the strong and solid foundation on which they built not only a business but a family. A legacy that tells a story whose ending is yet to be written, but a story that undeniably begins in a small corner market where people once gathered to talk and sip coffee. A place where people cared for one another. Where customers came to shop for what they needed but left with so much more than what they purchased.

These memories served as my compass, my grounding. They told me what I must do.

If these humble beginnings are what led me to become a misfit chef, then I proudly wear the title as a badge of honor—it has served me well. I have made an entire career out of not just making food but *sharing food with people*.

Which is exactly what this book is for.

My experience with food extends all the way back to my grandparents' tiny market and all the way into my kitchen today. And I invite you in. Welcome. Share some of my absolute favorite creations,

> My grandfather's butcher block stood straight and sturdy throughout all the years of his work, and under all the conversations my grandparents had with every customer.

recipes that I have developed, adapted, and honed throughout the years. Pull up a seat, pour a glass of wine, and hear stories of how food and people have influenced my life and about the experiences that have shaped me as a chef and as a person. And maybe, along the way, you'll discover how food has influenced *your* life.

And now, one very basic starting point:

I sincerely hope to impress upon you that cooking doesn't have to be scary, it doesn't have to be fancy or labor intensive—it only needs to be genuine and earnest. Every recipe that follows is something you can achieve, something you can perfect and even adapt to become your own. Better still, it can become a meal you can share.

Whoever you are—no matter your level of experience in the kitchen—you too can cook wonderful meals for others and create moments that matter.

So here we go. The following pages offer food and memories that have made me who I am, notions passed from generation to generation, perhaps tweaked a little here and there, yet as strong and sturdy as my grandfather's butcher block.

My grandfather Libby with my uncle, Joe, behind the butcher block at my grandparents' butcher shop / grocery store in East Boston, MA

SETTING THE TABLE

PART I

Into the Abyss

Horse pastures, orchards, fresh seafood markets.

The quaint hamlet of Ipswich, a small town on the North Shore of Massachusetts, is only about thirty miles north of my old neighborhood in East Boston—but for scenery, it's a galaxy away.

Established in 1634, Ipswich boasts more First Period homes than any other town in America: roofs at odd angles, hulking central chimneys, each house proudly sporting an official placard declaring the year the house was built. (*1812*: unimpressive. *1760*: ordinary. *1640*: esteem worthy.)

Quintessential New England. A place where neighbors meet on a downtown street with a "How ahh ya?" Don't be surprised to hear someone ask, "Who's ya fathah?" Families here stretch back to colonial times. *Gentrification* is still a dirty word.

But now, this quirky old town is home.

Time and distance from my grandparents' little market on Lexington Street brought myriad changes. I met Bob, we married, we adopted our first son. I left my post as director of performing arts at Suffolk University and graduated from Cambridge School of Culinary Arts' Professional Chef's Program. I settled into a new role as a stay-at-home dad, changing diapers and building LEGO masterpieces, only occasionally cooking for one-off catering jobs.

Yet my passion—for food and how it can bring people together—never wavered. In fact, quite the opposite. It intensified.

Until here I was, driving our five-year-old to school, but *not* simply sailing past the pastures and orchards and seafood markets. Today I was *stoked*. Because after our usual school-day drop-off routine—a stop at Dunks (coffee for Dad in the front seat, donut for Alex in the back seat), car stereo blaring, both of us bellowing—I would be making my first solo visit to Christopher's Table.

Actually, at the moment, it was really just an empty space, newly leased . . . but it was about to become my very own prepared-food shop.

Today, finally, I would step into the space alone—no leasing agents, landlords, or realtors—and start making the dream come true.

But as father and son sang our tunes, I couldn't help but notice something . . . *off*.

Alex seemed a little subdued.

I turned the music down and asked what was wrong. He was reluctant at first, but eventually he came around.

"I don't know what's going to happen," he said, and I could hear a five-year-old's anxiety in his voice.

I nudged him to explain. Finally, the truth came out.

"We have to get up in front of the class and talk about our art project."

Ah yes. Weeks ago, at parents' night, we'd heard about this project from Mrs. Bates, Alex's preschool teacher. She gave the students paintings by various famous artists—O'Keefe, Matisse, Van Gogh—but rendered in black-and-white outlines, coloring-book style. The children would color them in, then present their work to the class and talk about their reasons for the approach they'd taken.

No problem. Alex was a chatty kid. He generally had plenty to say! Alex talked to just about anyone who'd listen: grandmas in the grocery store, servers in restaurants, even the teenager in the drive-up window at Dunks.

"What are you worried about, buddy?" I asked gently.

"I don't know," he muttered. "What if . . . I *mess up*?"

"Alex, you can't mess this up," I replied with a smile. "There is no wrong answer."

Silence from the back seat.

"You got this, kiddo," I assured him. "We color together all the time. You can talk about that, right?"

His voice was strangely passive. "Yeah."

I knew this boy—and I knew he could talk about this art project, or anything else for that matter, for *hours*.

It was his fear of the unknown that was bothering him.

Of course, like any parent, I did my best to bolster his confidence, point out the positives, ease his fears. After a bit, Alex seemed to regain his pep. Soon we were belting out our morning music again, and by the time we rolled up at the school, it seemed all was well. I kissed him and hugged him; "You're gonna do great!" He gave me a lopsided smile and bounded off to the school door, backpack bouncing behind him.

Okay, morning parenting done. Now, on to the big event! My store!

As I approached Depot Square, in the heart of Ipswich, I was jittery with butterflies—but I couldn't keep from grinning like a schoolboy.

My dream was finally coming true.

I'd worked hard in my training, building my experience as a chef. I'd listened to my business adviser's every word. Now it was time for me to open my own place.

I parked at the curb and took a deep breath. Here I was, outside the prime real estate that would soon be my own shop. Suddenly now, all those daydreams, those crazy ideas, the irrepressible scenes I'd been staging in my head, had an anchor in reality. It was right there in front of me.

The store's lower story was brick fronted, with two large windows. The second level was wood shingled, painted white. I looked up at the previous tenant's sign still hanging there and imagined my own shiny new sign. Deep orange, with bright white lettering—*Christopher's Table: fine and prepared foods*—in a red frame and featuring the icon of a big red fork.

Elated, I walked up to the door, turned the key, and placed my hand on the cold handle. *This is it,* I thought. *This is really happening.*

I stepped into the store and breathed it in. The morning light poured in from the storefront's big windows. In that moment, I was transported to my childhood, the sun streaming into my grandparents' store all those years ago.

Which was no surprise, really, because so many of my ideas about my new shop—how it would look, how it would feel—stemmed from my memories of growing up at Millie's Market.

Now, as I looked around, my mind began filling the space. It wasn't just a matter of filling up the emptiness. It wasn't empty. The previous occupant had actually left plenty of items behind. Glasses hung above the bar, powdered gray with dust, as though the owner just slipped out for a bottle of wine one night and never came back. Miscellaneous pots and pans sat discarded in the kitchen. In the basement, water-stained shelves sagged, laden with broken Christmas decorations, some moldy.

There's a certain eeriness to being alone in a previously inhabited space, with marks of long-gone beings all around you. As I explored, a hint of unease mingled with my excitement.

But I was determined—I was looking forward to putting my own stamp on this place. The refit was already clear in my mind. Cleaning. Painting. Some minor carpentry. I liked thinking of opening my store as a blank page. I wanted to write my own story . . . and share it with my future customers.

I wanted to create a space where food could be *social*, like it was in my grandparents' store. I wanted everything about the store, its very *atmosphere*, to speak to that goal.

At the center of it all, I had made a key decision: for Christopher's Table to live up to its name, I would need to get myself a table!

But it couldn't be just any table.

It must serve as a showpiece for the store, front and center, a display table—indeed, worthy of its own display!

I searched for the perfect one. I visited dozens of furniture stores. Nothing felt right. Too small, too modern, too shiny and new. They had no story. I needed a table with history.

In Essex, Massachusetts—antiquing mecca of the universe,

population 3,600, with dozens of antique shops—I planned to rummage through a number of vintage stores.

But the rummaging never happened, because no sooner had I pulled into the parking lot of my very first stop than I saw it—just waiting there for me.

On the front porch of the store stood an old wooden table, wide, with strong, solid legs. I approached . . . ran my hand over the rough grain. I could feel where it had been hand planed, and where decades of use had worn parts of the surface.

I took out my tape measure and checked the dimensions. *It was perfect.* Inside the store, I rushed to find the proprietor . . . who told me the story.

A woodworker, blessed with a wife and six children, had made this table out of necessity to feed such a large brood. I loved the idea of my new table, the namesake of my restaurant, having such a history, serving such a noble purpose. I imagined the meals that had taken place around this table, the stories shared, the celebrations hosted. The woodworker's children had grown and gone; he and his wife were looking to downsize . . . so here it had ended up, in this shop. And now it was coming with me, for its next chapter.

We agreed on a price, arranged delivery. And the table's new life began.

It would become much more than a simple showpiece bearing the name of my store. This table would become the setting for countless events and shared meals, playing host to wine dinners, cooking classes, and children's cupcake-decorating parties. By adopting this simple piece of furniture, I was, in a way, carrying on its original, very social purpose. And this table as a presence in my shop—much like the butcher block in my grandparents' store—augmented my ethos: it became the stage on which I would act out and retell the story my grandparents had taught me so many years earlier. *It's not just about food. It's about people.*

Even before it arrived, I was thrilled to make the table the keystone of my store. Knowing it was on its way gave me a sense that things were really coming together. My confidence was growing as I felt my long-anticipated dream finally coming to fruition.

Beyond the dining area, through a swinging door, was a kitchen with plenty of space, a nice-sized walk-in refrigerator, and enough room for shelving to hold plenty of equipment and dry goods.

On the far side of the kitchen was an old wooden staircase leading down to the basement. On the other side was a thick, ominous metal door. I slid back the bolt and heaved the door open; there I found an identical old wooden staircase leading down to the basement—identical except that it contained even more cobwebs and dust.

You can't investigate all the nooks and crannies on a walk-through with a realtor. So I was curious, I guess a little determined, to check out this mysterious "other staircase." But before I could go squinting into the basement gloom, someone began banging on the front door.

Gas man. Coming to install the hookups for my stoves.

I hurried to meet him at the door, a tall, large man, older than me, with a serious face. He wore one of those blue work shirts, the kind with a patch for your name: his read *Mike*.

My guidance was simple: "Stoves here, gas meters here." He disappeared into the basement—*my* basement!—and I turned my attention back to the other set of wooden stairs, behind the thick metal door.

Yes, there was a light switch at the top of the stairs. Good. Flicked it—nothing. Not good.

What I could see and what I could hear did not quite compute. I thought I could hear Mike scuffling in the basement—which I assumed was the same basement into which I was about to descend—but as I peered down into the abyss, there was nothing but darkness. Absolutely no light.

Was there a separate offset basement? The passionate about-to-be shop owner immediately wondered, *Maybe even more storage for dry goods?*

I took a careful step into the darkness below. The old wood creaked like an angry cat. Every step was a new complaint. Of course I ignored the complaints. *I'm the tenant here! I'm a prepared-food shop owner!*

And the next step cracked like lightning.

The wood beneath me gave way to . . . thin air.

My body heaved awkwardly as I tumbled into the inky chasm.

In that split second when you're surprised and plunging into an uncertain future, there's a switch in your brain that gets flicked automatically, and suddenly you're in slow-mo.

You can even rewind and review.

Yes, look, there I am, lowering my weight onto that step, no worries.

Yes, there I am, plummeting through something like a scene from *Indiana Jones*.

Yes, I was wondering, in that moment, *What will I land on?*

Oh look! Here's how Chris looks when he wants to scream but no sound will come out—except that it's pitch black, so in reality you can't see him.

Was that metal door bolted shut for a reason?

Why did I decide to go down these stupid steps?

The brain is a marvelous organ. It can process a million questions in a millisecond.

Of course, it may not be able to *answer* those questions, but I digress.

I flailed. As I fell, I stretched my hands out before me, trying to break my fall. The sound of me hitting the ground—not pleasant. It was like dropping a steak on the floor, which no chef ever wants to do. Then the sound of glass breaking.

And then, there I was. Lying on cold concrete. Everything still. I forced my eyes open, then forced them open wider, trying to adjust to the blackness around me, hoping to reveal my surroundings.

Both my palms were scraped and stinging. Ah, maybe this explains the sound of glass breaking.

My head—yes, there was impact. (Thinking, thinking.) I was dizzy.

Oh, and nauseous.

Did I reach for my phone? I did not. Why? Because I never carry my phone. I am notorious for leaving my phone anywhere, everywhere. My phone was not in my pocket. There was no phone to reach for.

My heart rate spiked. My breathing quickened. I looked up at the lighted silhouette of a doorway at the top of what used to be a staircase.

"Mike!" I cried, without thinking, my voice cracking. *Thank heaven I saw his name tag!* "Mike!"

I was coming back to some semblance of reality. I was beginning to realize I was alive. Even as I called out to my gas man–savior, I was mentally checking my body to make sure all the parts were still there.

I could hear Mike moving toward the top of the stairs. His imposing frame stepped into view in the muted light above.

"Holy shit," he said.

He seemed to lean forward, as if to take a step.

"Stop!" I squawked. "The stairs are broken!"

How did Mike manage to get down to me? I have no idea. Maybe he clung to the banister still attached to the wall. But soon I could feel his large hand take hold of my arm. He pulled me up off the floor, helped me get back on my feet.

In the meager light of the open door above, I could see my hands. They were bleeding. I started to panic. I was in a flurry—heart racing, synapses firing. Mike handed me a rag for my hands. "Are you all right?" he asked. "What happened? Do you need to go to a hospital?"

Did I answer any of his questions? I can't remember. All I remember is the shame. *I'm a brand-new business owner, and I just landed on my ass. Maybe it was my head, I don't know.*

I urgently wanted to pretend it never happened.

Somehow, Mike and I both got back up out of the basement.

I was rattled, semishocked, my brain overcompensating, trying to take everything in and make sense of a moment I had no control over.

Then, suddenly, there was something I needed to take control over.

"I'm gonna be late," I blurted to Mike. "I gotta go pick up my kid. Do you mind locking the door behind you when you've finished?"

I didn't wait for his response.

As I got behind the wheel, I forced myself to calm down. Deep breath—more like a frenetic sneeze—then another deep breath. Deep breath, gulp, collect yourself, another deep breath.

Finally I took a quick succession of short breaths and turned the key to start the car.

Skreeeech!

Ah, the car was already running. "You idiot!"

I closed my eyes and shook my hands in the air, clearing the muddled slate, distancing myself from the frenzy. I checked my mirror, signaled to traffic as I pulled out of my parking spot; no, those are the windshield wipers; no, those are your high beams—"Shit!"

There it is, you got this.

Christopher's Table, day one.

My anxieties were pinging as I drove. My feeble little mantra, "You're okay, you're okay," was pointless. I gripped the steering wheel more tightly to hide from myself the fact that my hands were shaking.

I'm not okay.

The morning's back seat tensions, Alex's tensions, had moved to the front seat. Now they were bigger. They were mine.

The anxiety and fear and uncertainty of opening my own business, the nightmare of falling into the unknown, landing in pain in the darkness, it was all welling up inside me and spilling over.

I knew what I wanted to do—Christopher's Table! The dream!—but I was crippled by the fear of the unknown.

I sat in my car and wept. My Alex had felt his own version of this.

I don't know what's going to happen. What if I mess up?

It wasn't Alex's voice now. It was my own.

The unknown can be a horrible thing.

I didn't have such a ferocious need to open Christopher's Table, at that moment. I needed to give my son a hug.

At the school, I parked as usual, made my way to the front door as usual.

"Daddy!"

It was music to me.

Here was Alex, blue backpack bouncing behind him as he ran.

He charged straight into me, and I hugged him, and hugged him, and hugged him. I didn't want to let go—so I didn't.

The art project? The presentation? The talk to the class?

"Uh, good." He shrugged. "What's for supper?"

Uncertainty is everywhere.

We do our best to diminish it—with lighthearted affirmations, preschool projects about favorite colors, even antique dining tables. But it's still there. And there's no predicting how it will affect us.

As I write these words, Alex is not that five-year-old kid in the back seat. He's studying at the University of Vermont. He's had his share of school presentations, and he'll have a million more. He has faced many uncertainties and lived to see them through.

I have also survived the uncertainty of opening a business, of falling headfirst into darkness, of getting my share of bumps and scrapes.

The toil of opening and operating Christopher's Table resulted in years of full bellies and smiles, fantastic reviews and awards, and perhaps best of all, the knowledge that I succeeded in creating a quiet homage to my grandparents . . . turning a simple prepared-food shop into a place where a community was not only fed but built and sustained.

If we don't try, the result is always failure. So we get up in front of the classroom, or we open a shop—we face the unknown. We try.

Even when cooking from a new recipe, *not getting it right* is just part of the process.

The challenge isn't in getting it right. The challenge is adapting when we get it wrong.

Yes, we almost certainly will get it wrong. But that's what aprons are for.

I'm a misfit chef. Here's my philosophy: Go, be a mad scientist in the kitchen. Cook with reckless abandon. Discover things through fortunate failures.

Don't worry about the stuff you can't control, the uncertainties and the unknowns. Just try!

Bob and I were in the adoption queue, waiting and hoping for a second child.

Christopher's Table was still being built out, almost finished but still a mess, when I got the call.

"Lucas is ready for you. The adoption is finalized. You can come get him."

I stood up amid the construction mayhem and said—either to myself or aloud, I can't remember—"My water just broke. I have to go."

I am a witness: kids, even when they're only a few months old, have a way of focusing your attention.

Coconut Cupcakes with Cream Cheese Frosting

I remember baking batches of these cupcakes the night before we opened the doors of Christopher's Table—they were the very first items placed into our bakery case on opening day. They still conjure up excitement and anticipation all these years later.

Cupcakes:

- ¾ pound (3 sticks) unsalted butter
- 2 cups sugar
- 4 large eggs, room temperature
- 2 teaspoons pure vanilla extract
- 1 teaspoon pure almond extract
- 2½ cups flour
- 1 teaspoon baking powder
- ½ teaspoon baking soda
- ½ teaspoon kosher salt
- 1 cup buttermilk, shaken
- 1 (14-ounce) bag sweetened shredded coconut, divided

Frosting:

- 1 pound cream cheese, room temperature
- ¾ pound (3 sticks) unsalted butter, room temperature
- 1 teaspoon pure vanilla extract
- 1 teaspoon pure almond extract
- 4 cups confectioners' sugar

Makes 24 cupcakes

Preheat the oven to 325°F.

In the bowl of an electric mixer fitted with a paddle attachment, cream the butter and sugar on medium-high until light and fluffy, about 5 minutes. With the mixer on low speed, add the eggs, one at a time, scraping down the bowl after each addition. Add the vanilla and almond extracts and mix well.

In a separate bowl, mix the flour, baking powder, baking soda, and salt. In three parts, alternating, add the dry ingredients and the buttermilk to the butter mixture, beginning and ending with the dry ingredients. Mix until just combined. Fold in 7 ounces of the coconut.

Line a muffin pan with paper liners. Fill each liner to the top with batter. Bake for 25 minutes, or until the tops are brown and a tester comes out clean.

Allow the cupcakes to cool in the pan for 15 minutes, then remove them from the pan and cool completely on a cooling rack.

Meanwhile, make the frosting. In the bowl of an electric mixer fitted with a paddle attachment, cream the cream cheese, butter, and vanilla and almond extracts on low speed until combined. Add the confectioners' sugar and mix until smooth.

Frost the cupcakes and sprinkle the remaining 7 ounces of coconut on top.

Christopher's Chocolate Cake

At Christopher's Table we sold this decadent cake in gigantic slices. Nothing makes me feel more like a kid again than a slice of this cake and an ice-cold glass of milk.

Cake:
- 1¾ cups all-purpose flour
- 2 cups sugar
- ¾ cup cocoa powder
- 2 teaspoons baking soda
- 1 teaspoon baking powder
- 1 teaspoon kosher salt
- 1 cup buttermilk, shaken
- ½ cup vegetable oil
- 2 large eggs, room temperature
- 1 teaspoon pure vanilla extract
- 1 cup freshly brewed hot coffee

Frosting:
- ¼ pound (1 stick) unsalted butter, room temperature
- 2⅔ cups of confectioners' sugar
- 1 teaspoon pure vanilla extract
- 6 tablespoons whole milk
- ½ cup cocoa powder

Makes 8-10 servings

Preheat the oven to 350°F.

Butter two 8-inch round cake pans. Line the pans with parchment paper, then butter and flour the pans.

In the bowl of an electric mixer fitted with a paddle attachment, mix the flour, sugar, cocoa powder, baking soda, baking powder, and salt on low speed until combined.

In another bowl, combine the buttermilk, oil, eggs, and vanilla. With the mixer on low speed, slowly add the wet ingredients to the dry. With the mixer still on low, add the coffee and stir just to combine, scraping the bottom of the bowl with a rubber spatula.

Pour the batter evenly into the prepared pans and bake for 35 to 40 minutes, until a cake tester comes out clean. Cool in the pans for 30 minutes, then turn the cakes out onto a cooling rack and cool completely.

For the frosting, mix the butter and confectioners' sugar with an electric mixer on medium until smooth. Add the vanilla and milk. Slowly add the cocoa powder and mix until smooth and creamy. Add more milk to achieve the desired consistency.

Place one layer of the cake, flat side up, on a cake pedestal. With a knife or offset spatula, spread a thin layer of buttercream on the top only. Place the second layer on top, flat side up, and spread the frosting evenly first on the sides and then on the top.

Cut into wedges and serve at room temperature.

Perfect Chicken Salad

I grew up eating this chicken salad—it's my mom's recipe. Either by the pound or in a sandwich, this was a top seller at Christopher's Table.

3 boneless, skinless chicken breasts
1 cup celery, chopped
½ cup walnuts, chopped
1 cup red seedless grapes, sliced in half
1 cup mayonnaise*

*I swear by Cains mayonnaise

Makes 6 servings

Preheat the oven to 350°F.

If the chicken breasts are thick, slice them in half lengthwise to ensure even cooking. Place the chicken on a sheet pan and season generously with salt and pepper. Bake for 25 minutes, or until the chicken reaches an internal temperature of 165°F on a food thermometer. Let cool.

Combine the celery, walnuts, and grapes in a medium bowl.

When the chicken is cool enough to handle, slice it thinly to achieve a shredded texture. Add the chicken to the celery mixture.

Add the mayonnaise and mix well. Season to taste with salt and pepper.

Oven-Fried Chicken

I love the idea of fried chicken but not the process of deep-frying it. This recipe provides delicious crispy chicken without the mess (or extra calories) of frying.

- 1¼ cups buttermilk
- ¼ cup extra-virgin olive oil
- 3 tablespoons sriracha or similar hot sauce
- 2 tablespoons Dijon mustard
- 3 garlic cloves, minced
- 2 teaspoons salt, divided
- ½ teaspoon pepper
- 1 large onion, sliced
- 12 chicken pieces (breasts, thighs, and drumsticks) with skin and bones
- 2 cups dry unseasoned breadcrumbs
- ⅓ cup freshly grated Parmesan cheese
- ¼ cup all-purpose flour
- 2 teaspoons dried thyme
- 2 teaspoons paprika
- ½ teaspoon cayenne pepper
- 6 tablespoons butter, melted

Makes 6 servings

Whisk the buttermilk, oil, hot pepper sauce, mustard, garlic, 1 teaspoon of the salt, and pepper in a large bowl until well blended.

Add the sliced onion, then the chicken, and turn to coat. Refrigerate, covered, for at least 3 hours or up to 24 hours, turning the chicken occasionally.

Preheat the oven to 425°F.

Line two large rimmed baking sheets with parchment.

Whisk together the breadcrumbs, cheese, flour, thyme, paprika, cayenne, and remaining 1 teaspoon salt in a large baking dish.

Remove the chicken pieces from the marinade, allowing the excess to drip off. Add the chicken to the breadcrumb mixture and turn to coat completely.

Arrange the chicken, skin side up, on the baking sheets.

Drizzle the butter over the chicken. Bake until crisp, golden, and cooked through, 45 to 50 minutes. Serve warm or at room temperature.

Jam Thumbprint Cookies

These cookies are another one of my mom's recipes, except she rolled hers in crushed walnuts. At Christopher's Table we substituted coconut for the nuts.

¾ pound (3 sticks) unsalted butter, room temperature
1 cup sugar
1 teaspoon pure vanilla extract
3 cups all-purpose flour
¼ teaspoon kosher salt
1 egg beaten with 1 tablespoon water, for egg wash
1 bag sweetened flaked coconut
Raspberry or strawberry jam

Makes 32 cookies

In an electric mixer fitted with a paddle attachment, beat together the butter and sugar on low until they are just combined, then add the vanilla and mix well.

In another bowl, sift together the flour and salt. With the mixer on low speed, add the flour mixture to the butter and sugar. Mix until the dough starts to come together.

Dump the dough out onto a floured board and roll it into a flat disc. Wrap the dough in plastic wrap and refrigerate for 30 minutes.

Preheat the oven to 350°F.

Remove the dough from the plastic wrap. Roll the dough into 1¼-inch (1-ounce) balls.

Dip each ball into the egg wash and then roll it in the coconut.

Place the balls on an ungreased cookie sheet and press a light indentation into the top of each with your thumb. Drop ¼ teaspoon of the jam into each indentation.

Bake for 20 to 25 minutes, until the coconut is golden brown. Cool and serve.

Note: For ease, I place my jam in a squeeze bottle and fill the cookies that way.

Christopher's Marinated Steak Tips

These steak tips were so popular, I remember a customer who used to come in with his young son and buy the whole tray right out of the case. That "young son" is now a full-grown man, and he recently confessed that he still dreams of the steak tips from Christopher's Table.

1½ pounds prime steak tip, cut into large cubes
1 cup ketchup
1 cup Ken's Steak House Italian Dressing and Marinade
1 cup Coca-Cola

Makes 4–6 servings

Allow the steak to come to room temperature.

Season the steak cubes generously with salt and pepper.

Mix the ketchup, dressing, and cola in a bowl and whisk vigorously until well combined.

Place the steak tips in the marinade, making sure they are all submerged. Cover and refrigerate for 8 to 24 hours.

Preheat the grill to 400°F.

Allow the steak to come to room temperature while the grill is preheating.

Place the tips on the grill and cook uncovered for 6 to 8 minutes, until there are nice grill marks on the steak and it flips easily on the grill. Cook on all sides until it has reached the desired doneness, a total of 4 to 5 minutes more for medium rare.

Allow the steak tips to rest for 5 minutes, then serve.

Classic Whoopie Pies

When I was a kid growing up in New England, these treats were a staple in my house. They were a staple in the bakery case at Christopher's Table as well—jumbo size and filled with that sweet creamy filling.

1⅔ cups flour
⅔ cup unsweetened cocoa powder
1½ teaspoons baking soda
½ teaspoon kosher salt
4 tablespoons unsalted butter, room temperature
4 tablespoons vegetable shortening
1 cup brown sugar
1 large egg
1 teaspoon pure vanilla extract
1 cup whole milk
Classic Marshmallow Filling (recipe follows)

Makes 18–20 whoopie pies

Preheat the oven to 375°F.

Line two baking sheets with parchment paper.

Combine the flour, cocoa powder, baking soda, and salt.

In the bowl of a mixer fitted with a paddle attachment, cream the butter, shortening, and brown sugar on low speed until just combined. Increase the speed to medium and beat until fluffy. Add the egg and vanilla and beat for 2 to 3 minutes longer.

Add half the flour mixture and half the milk to the mixer and mix on low until incorporated. Add the remaining flour mixture and milk, scraping down the sides of the bowl. Beat until completely mixed.

Using a small ice cream scoop (or spoon), drop 1-tablespoon balls of batter onto the prepared baking sheets, leaving 2 inches between each. Bake one sheet at a time for 11 minutes, or until the cakes spring back when pressed.

Remove from the oven and let cool on the sheet for 5 minutes before moving the cakes to a wire rack to cool completely.

Put the marshmallow filling in a large pastry piping bag fitted with a star tip. Pipe a circle of filling around the perimeter of a whoopie pie half, then top it with a second whoopie pie half. Repeat until all the whoopie pies are assembled. Alternatively, you can use a small offset spatula to spread the filling.

Classic Marshmallow Filling

New Englanders will undoubtedly know that "Fluff" is that wonderful marshmallow spread made locally in Lynn, Massachusetts. If you're not lucky enough to have access to this lunch box staple, you can substitute a marshmallow alternative . . . or just relocate.

1½ cups Marshmallow Fluff
1¼ cups vegetable shortening
1 cup confectioners' sugar
1 tablespoon pure vanilla extract

Makes 2½ cups

In the bowl of a stand mixer fitted with a paddle attachment, beat the marshmallow fluff and vegetable shortening, starting on low and increasing the speed to high, until the mixture is smooth and fluffy, 3 to 5 minutes.

Reduce the speed to low and add the confectioners' sugar and vanilla, beating until incorporated. Increase the mixer speed to high and beat until fluffy, about 3 minutes.

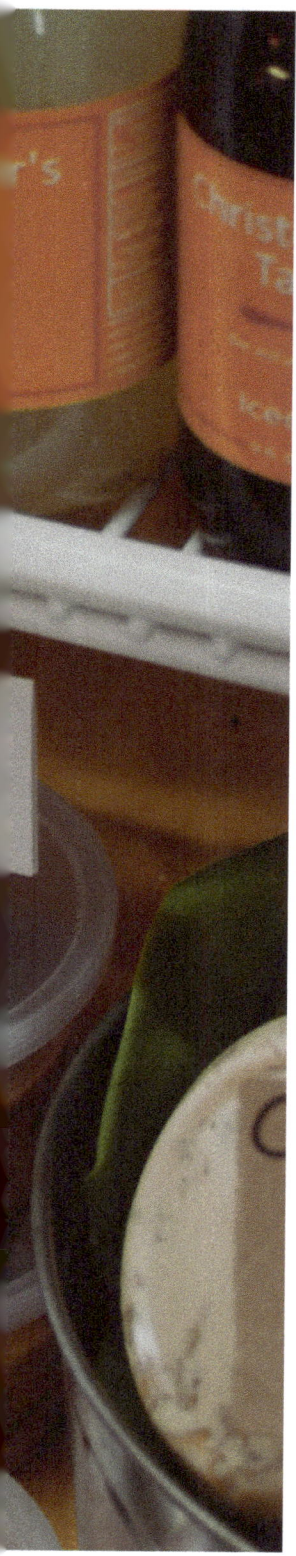

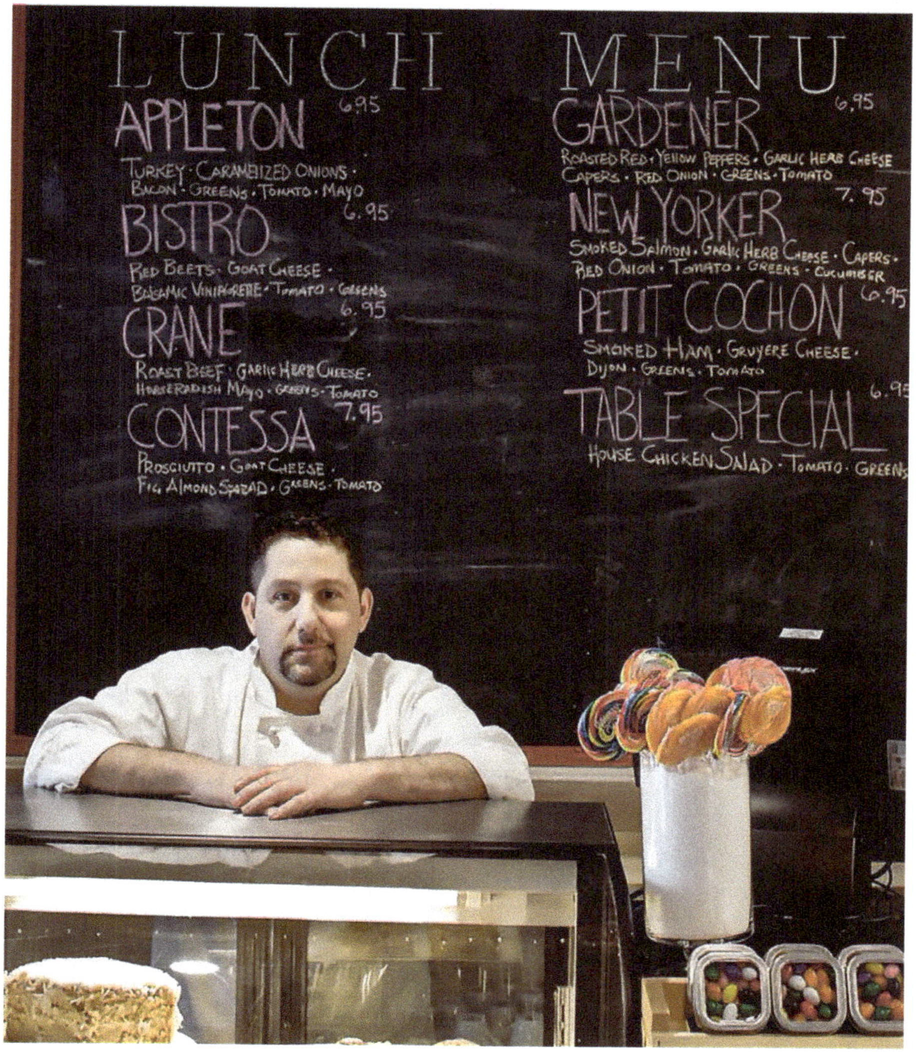
LUNCH MENU
APPLETON 6.95
TURKEY · CARAMELIZED ONIONS ·
BACON · GREENS · TOMATO · MAYO
BISTRO 6.95
RED BEETS · GOAT CHEESE ·
BALSAMIC VINAIGRETTE · TOMATO · GREENS
CRANE 6.95
ROAST BEEF · GARLIC HERB CHEESE ·
HORSERADISH MAYO · GREENS · TOMATO
CONTESSA 7.95
PROSCIUTTO · GOAT CHEESE ·
FIG ALMOND SPREAD · GREENS · TOMATO
GARDENER 6.95
ROASTED RED · YELLOW PEPPERS · GARLIC HERB CHEESE
CAPERS · RED ONION · GREENS · TOMATO
NEW YORKER 7.95
SMOKED SALMON · GARLIC HERB CHEESE · CAPERS ·
RED ONION · TOMATO · GREENS · CUCUMBER
PETIT COCHON 6.95
SMOKED HAM · GRUYERE CHEESE ·
DIJON · GREENS · TOMATO
TABLE SPECIAL 6.95
HOUSE CHICKEN SALAD · TOMATO · GREENS

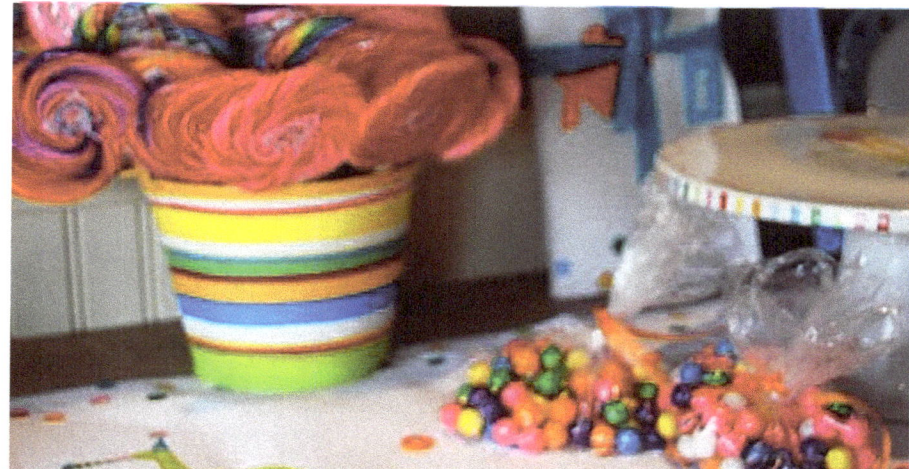

SEE WHAT STICKS

PART II

Here, Let Me Show You

Throw things against the wall and see what sticks.

That's been my approach from the beginning.

I wasn't an ordinary chef, and I wasn't an ordinary businessperson. I knew (a) I loved food and (b) I wanted to share it and (c) I needed to make enough money to live. I was cool with (a) and (b). But to get to (c), I experimented.

So I looked around at my little world. At the store, you came in, you chose a product, you gave me money for it, and you left. It wasn't a process that would happen automatically, nor a process that could totally fund my life. Many a small business owner has learned the hard way that you can't simply sit back and wait for customers to come waltzing in.

What could I do to embellish, to augment, this "shop in my little store" process? It would need to be something that made sense. That fit. Something that remained true to (a) and (b). Yes, I could have started selling cocaine out of my walk-in fridge (like some people in other restaurants I've worked in). Probably would have been way easier, and more profitable! But of course that wasn't what Christopher's Table was meant to be. It wasn't true to *me*.

Cooking classes felt right.

This wasn't merely about (c)—it wasn't just about making money. It was also a reaction to the reality of small business ownership: in the early days especially, between customers, I was alone in the store a lot of the time. For me, it wasn't about "selling classes" any more than it was about food. It was about *people*.

I went in each morning, by myself, and made muffins. Cookies. Whoopie pies. Whatever. It was solitary. I put my lovely products in the case and waited for people to come in and buy them. But it wasn't the well-established store my grandparents had, one intricately intertwined with the neighborhood. It wasn't a hangout. For most of the day, except for a few interruptions of varying numbers of minutes, I was alone.

Cooking classes meant *people*. The heart of the vision. What Christopher's Table was intended to be. Cooking classes were, for me, a way *to not be lonely*. To escape the isolation of the kitchen. A way to open the door of that kitchen and invite people in.

It wasn't a matter of "sharing my superior knowledge." I'm not a sophisticate. I'm actually a grown-up version of the little schoolkid who loved potato chips more than any other food on earth. (To this day, I would push you in front of a bus for potato chips.) My culinary journey began on the playground at Saint Mary Star of the Sea school in East Boston, where the Italian slush truck pulled up every day during recess. Other kids bought all different flavors of slushies, but I'd buy a bag of chips and a bag of M&M's, then dump the M&M's in on top of the chips. The candies would fall to the bottom of the bag. While the other kids were playing basketball or tag, I was standing off to the side indulging in my culinary masterpiece: eating only the chips, then luxuriating in the M&M's covered in grease and salt! That sweet-salty combination launched my love of experimenting with flavors.

And I was still experimenting even as I was teaching. The truth is, I often found myself saying, "I don't know. Let's figure it out together." In a Christopher's Table cooking class, it was more important that we were all *there*, having fun, drinking wine, *connected*. I'm not a scholar. I've never had any interest in teaching people how to properly sauté sofrito. No. I want fifteen people in my kitchen with glasses sloshing and someone saying, "What? You want me to butterfly this pork tenderloin? What does that even *mean*?"

And as I demonstrate, we're laughing.

No, I'm probably not demonstrating in a manner acceptable to any culinary-school teacher—but my students will be able to go home and do it. "Slice across, open it up, rub with garlic, butter, rosemary, roll it back up, tie it with string . . . and it's gonna be delicious!"

That was the whole point of my cooking classes. They allowed me to—for lack of a better word—play. My kitchen became a playground. With, and for, other kids!

These "other kids" could be anybody.

I was still in elementary school when a new family moved in across the street from our apartment above the grocery store. They had a boy named Eric, about my age. We became friends pretty quickly. Shortly thereafter, when my parents were planning to throw a big Halloween party, predominantly for adults, they told me I could invite a friend so I'd have someone to hang out with during the event.

Without hesitating, I announced my choice: "I wanna invite the new kid across the street!"

My parents blanched. At the moment, young and clueless, I didn't perceive the reason. It wasn't until later that I connected the dots. Eric's father was white, his mother was Black. I wanted to invite the one biracial kid in the entire neighborhood. In those days, in East Boston, that could be an issue.

But to their credit, my parents approved the choice. Eric and I spent most of the night sitting under a table drinking punch, he in his C-3PO costume and me dressed as Elvis. We giggled as tipsy costumed adults danced around the room. Eric and I remained friends all the way through high school, and reconnected as adults via Facebook. He's married today, a successful musician, a bass player. He survived growing up Black in East Boston.

And I learned, firsthand, that diversity is a decision. Plenty of people will make judgments about someone on the basis of their skin color or their sexual orientation or their financial status or any number of other factors. But I could choose inclusion. I could celebrate people as *people*.

Cooking classes at Christopher's Table? The door was wide open. Everyone was welcome at this table!

So what do cooking classes entail? Not just food and people and tools. It's more complicated than that.

For one thing, it's promotion. You have to let people know that the classes are happening, and inspire them to be involved. In those days, everyone was on Facebook. There was little or no competition for that platform. So Facebook was my friend, and I was never very far away from my laptop. It was the equivalent of my grandmother's cash register. Virtually all my day-to-day business was conducted on this machine. (I sometimes said, to my own amazement, "I can make a cheesecake, take it out of the oven, post it on Facebook, and make $85 in twenty minutes.")

After serving as director of performing arts at Suffolk University for eight years, I was used to producing events. I brought that producer's approach to Christopher's Table. There was a theatrical aspect to it. How do we put all this together? How will it feel to the audience?

Okay, I'm gonna do a cooking class.

Details, details:

- I didn't have a liquor license at the time, so participants would be encouraged to bring their own wine or beer.
- I would charge a flat rate for each class.
- I knew the recipes I would feature, presenting each class around a theme in order to market them attractively.
- How many people could I get into my kitchen—I mean safely, with things like knives and fire—since these would be people who didn't necessarily know how to cook or even use a knife? And the size of the table was a significant factor: How many people could fit comfortably around this table? The endgame was not the

food; it was a bunch of people sitting around the table enjoying the meal. Beyond the food to what you do with it. Final answer—total capacity: fifteen people.

After these decisions were made, it was pretty easy: I put it out on Facebook, and kaboom.

The day soon came when the sign on the store's front door said *Christopher's Table will be closed tonight for a sold-out cooking class.*

In the front window stood the large, majestic namesake table, carefully set with fifteen identical place settings. Atop each plate, a neatly folded cloth napkin bearing a small menu card detailing the dishes the class would make.

The last remnants of the day's sun poured through the windows, spilled onto the table, ricocheted off the silver through polished wine glasses, and zigzagged in every direction across the room.

It wasn't long before locals grew accustomed to such a sign on the door. Cooking classes were a hit. Once or twice each month, participants arrived in pairs or small groups. Almost always women, local moms whose children went to school together or whose husbands golfed together on weekends. Sure, there was the occasional couple turning up for a date night, or the random student who really wanted to start eating healthier, arriving in search of good recipes, but they were the exceptions.

The regulars, the ones who signed up every month without fail, were women who simply craved a night out of their own. They turned simple culinary lessons into opportunities to catch up with friends and recharge—while drinking wine in the kitchen with me—and to meet new people.

It all happened over the span of an evening of cooking and imbibing, which ended with everyone gathered at the table together, new and old friends alike, sharing a meal they themselves created.

Look at history. At the heart of every movement or uprising can be found a group of instigators—change agents or simply individuals who believed in something so strongly that their enthusiasm, their passion, created infectious momentum. Likewise, I attribute much of the success and longevity of my cooking classes to a small group of women who seemed hell-bent on never missing a class: Carmella, Joan, Krista, and Sara—cooking class regulars, self-appointed groupies, who took it upon themselves to serve as lieutenants in my culinary army.

Almost always arriving early, they flattered me by more or less taking ownership of the whole process. They welcomed new participants and oriented them to the ins and outs of how the class worked. They generously offered instant camaraderie to all who showed up. Their energy was contagious.

- Joan, a single mom, one of the funniest people I've ever known.
- Sara, loud and wonderful, gregarious, a truly social animal.
- Her workmate Krista, a tall redhead invited by Sara to the very first cooking class, who instantly fit right in.
- And brassy Carmella, an intense Italian who could take on the world. "We're gonna make escargot? I don't even know what that is. Let's do it!"

It was like a sitcom: regular characters in every episode, but interwoven with occasional guests or cameos. Carmella's sister-in-law Tammy circulated in and out. Others came and went. But the fabulous foursome were the constant. As every class unfolded, I watched with joy as these four bubbly women transformed a table of strangers into a raucous, wine-toasting group of gal pals. Before each class, even as they stepped into the room, their triumphant announcement could be heard: "We're *here!*" They made their entrance as if they were guests of honor at their own party.

Then came Tom.

He put his hand tentatively on the doorknob and paused for a moment, reading the sign taped to the window. Through the double-doored entry, he could hear the volume of women's voices.

Sweat began to bead on the back of his neck, and he considered abandoning the idea and just turning around and going home.

But then, under his breath, he muttered, "Good grief," pulled the door open, and stepped inside.

Damn. He was the last to arrive.

Tom—maybe in his forties, thinning light-brown hair, average height, average build, average looks, a perfectly stereotypical Mr. Nice Guy—stood awkwardly staring at the table and the fourteen women surrounding it. With his hands stuffed deep into the pockets of his L.L. Bean field jacket, he reminded me of Charlie Brown. His eyes instantly locked with mine, and I could feel his silent, desperate cry for help.

"You must be Tom?" I asked cheerfully.

(My deductive reasoning wasn't all that impressive; his name was the only one remaining on the class roster, and I was the only other person in the room with XY chromosomes. But Tom was desperately grateful.)

"Wow! Hey, yeah, how'd you know that?" he asked earnestly.

In those first minutes, Tom couldn't leave my side. Without words, he seemed terrified and impressed at the same time. I showed him a drink list. "Can I bring you a glass of wine or beer?" He removed his hands from his pockets. As he perused the list, he began to nervously wring his hands like a cartoon supervillain. I pointed Tom to the one remaining seat. He turned and faced the long table—filled with wine and women—and like a teacher making an introduction on a late-arriving child's first day of school, I raised my voice above the din and shouted, "Hey, everyone, this is Tom!"

Tom survived.

Moving into the large commercial kitchen behind the storefront, I provided an overview of how the class would operate and outlined the recipes and ingredients we'd be working on together. The kitchen was divided into workstations, each outfitted for a specific recipe and course. I asked the class to break themselves up into small groups and choose a station.

I confess, it always made me anxious as these passionate women began to move around the kitchen, pairing up amid exclamations of "I want to work with dessert" or "Let's take the salad course, it seems the easiest!" Perhaps my childhood memories dogged me, always being picked last for sports teams—or maybe it was my fear that any given group of strangers simply wouldn't mesh well, in defiance of my dream of bringing people together—but in any case, I somehow dreaded this part of the class, watching anxiously until each participant was safely grouped at a station. In the end, everyone always found a place.

That first evening with Tom, however, he was . . . how shall I say this? A special case.

I saw from across the room that he remained motionless as the women swirled around him. His hands returned to his pockets, his shoulders rose to his ears. He looked something like a turtle retreating into his shell.

But before I could make a move to rescue Tom, Sara's voice trumpeted from the appetizer station: "Tom! Over here, Tom, come help us with the first course!"

In that instant, Tom and I both released a collective sigh of relief.

I'd like to believe it was a seminal moment, because from that night forward, Tom was inducted into the Joan-Sara-Carmella-Krista club of regulars. For close to two years, not a single

Tom and Sara in the kitchen for a cooking class at Christopher's Table in Ipswich, MA

cooking class went by that Tom did not join the women for a night of wine and cooking. Tom wasn't a culinary mastermind, but he tried hard. Actually, truth be told, I always knew that when Tom partnered with Sara in the kitchen, some sort of disaster would follow.

"Tom thinks his Band-Aid may have fallen into the soufflé batter."

"Our cake is in the oven, but Sara just realized she never put in the eggs."

Over time, we all learned the truth about Tom. He had initially come to my cooking class in search of something more than just a good recipe for seared salmon. He eventually admitted that he signed up for that first class in the hopes of meeting a nice woman to date. After which, the regulars began lovingly scanning the list of each class's participants for a potential match. Tom didn't find the love of his life in our classes, but he did acquire four loving sisters! The power of food, in action. His new sisters routinely swarmed him, eager to hear updates on his romantic adventures, always imparting dating tips—and they playfully ribbed him whenever he made a dating faux pas. What's she like? Where did you take her? Did you pick her up or meet her there? Why didn't you pick her up? *Well, she has a car.* It would've been nice if you picked her up! *Okay, I'll pick her up next time.* After dinner, did you walk her to her car? *I probably should have.* Oh, Tom!

Tom was ever hopeful of snaring a romantic partner, and improving his culinary skills was one way he imagined it could happen. He was inordinately impressed with me, so to his way of thinking, the more he could learn from my cooking classes, the better his chances of matrimonial bliss. He also had an outsized passion for salmon—he adored the salmon we served up at Christopher's Table—so he was thrilled in one class to see that we would be learning to sear salmon.

That evening, as I shook the pan, it caught some of the flame, and Tom was dazzled. This was the coolest thing he had ever seen. So he kept the recipe, determined to bring a date to his house for a dinner of seared salmon—where he intended to cook it *exactly the way Christopher did it!* The fire in the pan would be his money shot. He was sure that after she saw the flame lick up like that, she would fall hopelessly in love with him and they would marry and live happily ever after.

Tragically, the salmon didn't move. It stuck to the pan. No fire licked seductively up from the stove. His date did not fall in love with him. They did not marry and live happily ever after. Yes, the seared salmon was delicious, but no fire, no fantasy.

Sorry, Tom!

Did Edna start all this? Perhaps. Let's blame Edna.

There was a television show, *The Facts of Life*, set in an all-girls boarding school. The house mother, Mrs. Garrett, was played by a big, very funny, Rubenesque actor named Charlotte Rae. Over time, as the actors playing the high school students aged out of their roles, the storyline morphed. Mrs. Garrett—Edna—opened a gourmet prepared-food shop called Edna's Edibles. Cases filled with croissants and an array of other delightful delectables.

I wanted to be Edna.

In a cooking class one evening, well into multiple bottles of wine, I revealed this secret. I longed to be this kooky middle-aged woman named Edna! The women thought it was wonderful. The next morning, I pulled up to my store on Depot Square to find papers all over my front windows. My first response was panic. *The Ipswich Board of Health has condemned my business!* I got out of my car and studied the papers. They were promotional posters, designed and printed and posted by the fabulous foursome, reading *Coming Soon: Edna's Edibles*.

Funny, ladies, very funny.

Cooking classes were a wonderful antidote to my loneliness. I was a classic independent small business owner, which meant I was my own boss, with no board of directors, no business partner, no marketing manager, no one to say, "That's a terrible idea" or "You can't do an online raffle; it's against the law." It was just me. I had the advantage of no opposition, no conflict—but the disadvantage of no advice, no teamwork . . . no camaraderie.

For class themes, I had the freedom to choose whatever I wanted.

So I put on my marketing hat and chose themes that I felt people would get excited about. A Night in Tuscany! Ya gotta make it a little sexy, right? A Night in Thailand! I had some great Thai recipes from a trip I'd taken years before to Bangkok and Chiang Mai. An Italian night. An autumn comfort-food night. A springtime Cooking from the Garden night, based on whatever was in bloom.

I had no idea, when I began, how the classes would go over, and what frequency of classes could reliably sell out. If I could fill a class only every three months, they would have become quarterly. But it was evident early on that a class a month—or even two classes a month—would fill up absolutely every time. People were more than willing to pay $45 apiece—a pretty modest fee—and producing a class that grossed $675 didn't really cost me a lot. Later, when I obtained a beer and wine license, I moved from BYO to selling libations myself, and the classes produced even more revenue.

Some fifty times over the course of a few years, we gathered, we laughed, we learned, we drank, we ate, we enjoyed each other.

Well, most of us enjoyed each other, most of the time . . .

For one class, I welcomed a group of obviously affluent women from the neighboring town of Boxford. From the first moment, it was clear that the fabulous foursome didn't appreciate these characters. No, perhaps that's not a strong enough description. It was the Sharks and the Jets.

But fisticuffs were avoided, no lives were lost. When the Boxford group departed, the fabulous foursome descended on me with questions and opinions: "Who the hell were they?" "Where do they come from?" "Who do they think they are?" "They were snooty." "They were snobbish." "They were giving me the stink eye!" "That one woman doesn't even know how to hold a knife!"

Not exactly the model of inclusion that I had envisioned for Christopher's Table.

From that night on, with the announcement of each new class, Joan would ask the killer question: "Are those *Boxford ladies* coming?" To my secret relief, the answer was always no. I think the stink eye may have gone both ways. The fabulous foursome seemed to have scared off the Boxford ladies. But I could only smile and remind myself: There will always be opportunities for exclusion. Diversity is a decision you have to keep making every single day.

And as for our friend Tom? Years later, long after the final cooking class at Christopher's Table, I saw him again. He was still Charlie Brown. And still single.

Roast Pork Tenderloin with Poached Plums

This was a great recipe for cooking classes at Christopher's Table. It has simple ingredients and is easy to make, yet it produces a delicious and beautiful meal.

6 sweet, firm red or black plums, pitted and quartered
2 cups white wine (pinot gris or pinot grigio)
1 cup dry red wine
2 whole star anise
1 cinnamon stick
¼ cup plus 1¼ teaspoons sugar, divided
2 cups low-salt chicken broth
5 fresh thyme sprigs plus 1 teaspoon finely chopped thyme, divided
3 tablespoons chopped shallot
2 pork tenderloins (1 to 1½ pounds each)
3 tablespoons olive oil, divided
3 garlic cloves, minced
1 teaspoon kosher salt
1 teaspoon pepper

Makes 6 servings

Heat the plums, white wine, red wine, star anise, cinnamon stick, and ¼ cup of the sugar in a large heavy saucepan; bring to a boil, stirring until the sugar dissolves. Reduce the heat; simmer until the plums are tender, about 20 minutes.

Transfer the plums to a platter. Strain the wine mixture. Return the strained liquid to the same saucepan. Add the broth, 5 thyme sprigs, and shallot. Boil until the mixture is reduced to 1 cup, about 25 minutes.

Strain the sauce; stir in the remaining 1¼ teaspoons sugar and ½ teaspoon of the finely chopped thyme. Season with salt and pepper.

Preheat the oven to 400°F.

Rub the pork with 1 tablespoon of the oil, then sprinkle with the remaining ½ teaspoon thyme, garlic, salt, and pepper. Heat the remaining 2 tablespoons oil in a large ovenproof skillet over medium-high heat. Add the pork and sear until brown on all sides, turning often, about 5 minutes.

Transfer the skillet to the oven and roast the pork until a thermometer inserted into the center registers 140°F, about 20 minutes. Remove the skillet from the oven and let the pork stand for 10 minutes. Cut the pork crosswise into ½-inch-thick slices.

Serve with the poached plums and sauce.

Note: The poached plums can be made a day ahead. Cover the plums and sauce separately and refrigerate. To serve, bring the plums to room temperature and rewarm the sauce over medium heat.

Warm Arugula Salad with Caramelized Red Onion, Pancetta, and Pine Nuts

The salad course was always a safe bet for cooking class participants who were unsure of their abilities, but I always liked to give them a challenge of some sort. The caramelized red onion mix in this recipe was just the right amount of "push" they needed.

2 medium red onions
½ cup diced pancetta
3 tablespoons olive oil
4 fresh thyme sprigs
¼ cup pine nuts
5 cups arugula
Balsamic vinegar
Parmesan, for shaving

Makes 4 servings

Peel, halve, and quarter the onions, then quarter again, to give you 8 pieces from each onion. (Leave the root end intact to keep the onion from falling apart.)

Heat a frying pan and cook the pancetta until crisp. Add the olive oil, thyme, onions, pine nuts, and a pinch of salt to the pan. Toss around and cook on medium heat for about 8 minutes, until the onions are caramelized and sweet.

Toss the onion mixture with the arugula in a salad bowl.

Drizzle the salad generously with balsamic vinegar—this will make a natural dressing as it mixes with the olive oil. Serve with shaved Parmesan on top (you can use a potato peeler to shave the Parmesan).

Orecchiette with Sausage and Broccolini

Another cooking class favorite! It's simple, with just a few ingredients, yet yielding an amazing dish you'll make again and again. Orecchiette is little hat-shaped pasta that you can find in most larger grocery stores.

2 heads broccolini
1 pound orecchiette pasta
3 tablespoons olive oil
1 pound ground pork sausage (I use 3 hot Italian sausage links with the casings removed)
3 garlic cloves, minced
1 teaspoon red pepper flakes (optional)
½ cup grated Parmesan cheese

Makes 6 servings

Bring a pot of salted water to a boil. Cook the broccolini for 5 minutes or until crisp-tender. Remove the broccolini from the pot.

Cook the orecchiette in the broccolini water for 10 to 12 minutes, or until cooked through. Reserve 1 cup of the pasta water.

While the pasta is cooking, heat the oil in a frying pan over medium heat. Add the pork sausage, garlic, and red pepper flakes. Sauté until the pork is browned and cooked through and the garlic is fragrant and browned.

Add the cooked broccolini and orecchiette to the sauté pan and toss to coat with the pork mixture.

Remove the pan from the heat and add the reserved pasta water and grated cheese. Mix until the cheese melts and forms a sauce. Season with salt and pepper.

Tom's Date-Night Seared Salmon with Maple-Soy Glaze

Tom was a regular at the Christopher's Table cooking classes. He loved salmon, and this became his tried-and-true recipe at home whenever he was trying to win the attention of a special someone.

- 4 to 6 salmon fillets, 4 to 6 ounces each
- ½ teaspoon salt
- ¼ teaspoon pepper
- 1 tablespoon sesame oil
- 1 tablespoon unsalted butter
- 2 cloves garlic, minced
- 1 teaspoon fresh ginger, minced or grated
- ½ cup maple syrup
- 3 tablespoons low-sodium soy sauce
- Sesame seeds (garnish)
- 1 green onion, chopped (garnish)

Makes 4–6 servings

Season the salmon fillets on all sides with salt and pepper.

Heat the sesame oil in a skillet over medium heat. Cook the salmon for 4 to 5 minutes per side, or until golden brown and completely cooked through. Remove the salmon from the skillet.

Melt the butter in the skillet, then add the garlic and ginger. Sauté for 1 minute or until lightly browned. Add the maple syrup and soy sauce. Let the sauce bubble for 2 to 3 minutes, or until thickened slightly. It will thicken more as it cools.

Remove the skillet from the heat and return the salmon to the pan. Spoon the sauce over the salmon fillets to coat them. Garnish with sesame seeds and green onion to serve.

Crispy Polenta with Rosemary

I love polenta and I love anything crispy—this amazing recipe combines them both.

¼ pound unsalted butter plus more for frying
¼ cup olive oil plus more for frying
1 tablespoon minced garlic (3 cloves)
1 teaspoon red pepper flakes
2 teaspoons minced fresh rosemary
½ teaspoon kosher salt
½ teaspoon pepper
3 cups chicken stock
2 cups half-and-half
2 cups milk
2 cups yellow cornmeal
½ cup grated Parmesan cheese
Flour

Makes 8-10 servings

Heat the butter and olive oil in a large saucepan. Add the garlic, red pepper flakes, rosemary, salt, and pepper and sauté for 1 minute. Add the chicken stock, half-and-half, and milk and bring to a boil.

Remove from the heat and slowly sprinkle in the cornmeal while stirring with a whisk. Cook over low heat, stirring constantly, for a few minutes, until thickened and bubbly. The mixture should be smooth with no large lumps.

Remove the pan from the heat and stir in the Parmesan. Pour into a 9 x 13 x 2-inch pan, smooth the top, and refrigerate until the polenta is firm and cold.

Cut the chilled polenta into squares. Dust each square lightly in flour.

Heat 1 tablespoon olive oil and 1 tablespoon butter in a large sauté pan and fry the squares, in batches, over medium heat for 3 to 5 minutes, turning once, until browned on the outside and heated inside.

Chocolate-Dipped Almond Biscotti

Cookies were always a fun choice at our cooking classes. These Italian treats often showed up during our Taste of Italy-themed classes.

- 1¼ cups whole almonds, toasted
- 2 cups plus 1 tablespoon all-purpose flour, plus more for your hands
- 1 cup packed light brown sugar
- 1 teaspoon baking powder
- ½ teaspoon ground cinnamon
- ½ teaspoon salt
- 4 tablespoons unsalted butter, cold and cubed
- 3 large eggs
- 1 tablespoon canola or vegetable oil
- 1 teaspoon pure vanilla extract
- 1 large egg beaten with 1 tablespoon milk, for egg wash
- 8 ounces semisweet chocolate, coarsely chopped

Makes 24 pieces

Preheat the oven to 350°F.

Pulse the toasted almonds in a food processor until they are very coarsely chopped. Set 1 cup of chopped toasted almonds aside. Pulse the remaining toasted almonds until they are finer in texture (you will sprinkle this on top of the chocolate later).

In a large mixing bowl, whisk together the flour, brown sugar, baking powder, cinnamon, and salt. Cut in the butter until the mixture is crumbly. Gently toss in the 1 cup of coarsely chopped almonds.

In a medium bowl, whisk together the eggs, oil, and vanilla. Pour the egg mixture into the flour mixture and gently stir with a large wooden spoon or rubber spatula until everything is just barely moistened.

Turn the dough out onto a lightly floured surface, and with floured hands, knead lightly until the dough is soft and slightly sticky, about 8 to 10 times. With floured hands, divide the dough in two and place each half onto a baking sheet. Shape each half into an 8- to 9-inch-long roll, patting them down until each is about ½ inch thick.

Using a pastry brush, lightly brush the top and sides of each biscotti slab with egg wash. Bake in batches (or together) for 25 to 26 minutes, or until the tops and sides of the biscotti slabs are lightly browned.

Remove from the oven, but do not turn off the heat. Allow the slabs to cool for 10 minutes. Once the slabs are cool enough to handle, cut each into 1-inch-thick slices. Place the slices with cut sides facing up ¼ inch

apart on baking sheets. Return to the oven and bake for 9 minutes.

Turn the biscotti over and bake the other sides for 9 minutes. The cookie centers will be slightly soft with harder edges. Remove from the oven and allow to cool for 5 minutes on the baking sheet. Then transfer the cookies to a wire rack to cool completely before dipping them in chocolate. Save the baking sheets for the next step. As the biscotti cools, it becomes crunchy.

Melt the chocolate in a medium bowl in the microwave, or use a double boiler. (The key to melting chocolate in the microwave is to do it in small bursts and stir frequently. Chocolate seizes so fast, so easily. Melt in 15-second increments, stirring vigorously with a spoon after each increment, until completely melted and smooth.)

Dip one side of each biscotti cookie in melted chocolate and immediately sprinkle with the remaining toasted almond crumbs. (I do this over the sink to avoid a mess!)

Place the dipped biscotti back on the baking sheets and allow the chocolate to set in the refrigerator or at room temperature, 30 to 45 minutes.

RECIPE: CHOCOLATE-DIPPED ALMOND BISCOTTI

PART III

FARM
FABULOUS

No Kitchen, No Problem

Preparing and serving a five-course dinner for more than a hundred people? No problem.

Making it happen out in a field, on a farm, with no stove, no running water, and no kitchen staff?

Well, it seemed like a good idea at the time.

Truth be told, while my cooking classes succeeded in bringing people into my little shop, a part of me still wanted to get out of the kitchen. Get out into the world. Get with people *out there*.

As Christopher's Table grew more and more popular with the locals and people were showing up from an ever-enlarging geographic area, I didn't grow more content. Quite the contrary: the success energized me, inspired me to keep trying new things . . . to keep our growing Christopher's Table family connected, to give them new adventures!

The vision for Dinner on the Farm didn't spring full blown into my mind in a flash. It came together gradually, and simmered for a long time. You might say its real genesis dates all the way back to the 1960s, when I was still a boy. American consumers in that era began complaining about the bland taste of processed foods. Like today, most restaurants were acquiring their produce from sources far away, even outside the country—ingredients that had to be shipped long distances, which meant they were often harvested before ripening to lengthen their lifespan. Result: food that was not only far less flavorful but also significantly less nutritious.

But when chef Alice Waters opened her restaurant Chez Panisse in Berkeley, California, in 1971, a farm-to-table (or farm-to-fork) movement began picking up speed. Restaurants began buying their ingredients from local and nearby sources, which meant far fresher-tasting and healthier dishes for their customers.

Which was an idea I loved. When the farm-to-table concept caught my attention, I swooned. With Christopher's Table doing well, I was free to dream . . . and I romanticized the idea of producing elaborate meals in a bucolic farm setting.

Ingredients were surely plentiful! The coastal communities of Massachusetts' North Shore are home to numerous small local farms and fisheries. I'd have easy access to freshly grown fruit, produce, dairy, and even meat. And as I relied on the support of my customers, I loved the notion of supporting, in turn, the farmers and food producers of my own local area. Obtaining fresh, high-quality ingredients and presenting them to my customers seemed like a win-win for everybody.

But here again, it wasn't just about the food. It was about the people. At the heart of farm to table is the idea of *forging relationships*. Maybe you've seen the bumper sticker: *Know Your Farmer*. We need to know where our food is coming from, and even better, who is producing it.

Which brought me to a scraggly-bearded, sun-browned young farmer named Noah.

It started with his mother, a classically trained musician I had the good fortune of meeting in my store. She showed up just like any other first-time customer, but before very long, she handed me a card—a move it felt like she had made in other venues many times before.

"You should give my son a call," she announced. Noah was the owner of Alprilla Farm in Essex, the next town over.

I called within a day, but I guess farmers don't carry their cell phones and drop everything to return calls. It was a while before Noah got back to me. "I don't know what you can do for me," I admitted. I really didn't know what to expect.

I couldn't have expected Noah.

Under a well-worn wide-brimmed straw hat, which shaded his

big, sandy, Amish-style beard, this possibly-20-year-old pulled up in front of Christopher's Table on a beat-up old Schwinn bicycle with a large milk crate bungeed to the back. Bursting from the milk crate were his wares: a unique assortment of carrots and fresh greens and who knows what.

Looks can be deceiving.

He had grown up on the farm, working the vegetable garden with his parents and helping with haying. The summer after high school graduation, he got a job at Appleton Farms, a big operation on the Ipswich-Topsfield line, and found himself—in his own words—"hopelessly addicted to farming." He studied sustainable agriculture at Hampshire College, put in a season of solo market gardening and an apprenticeship at Butterworks Farm in Vermont, then launched a new version of Alprilla Farm in partnership with a friend. Noah served—again, in his own words—as Alprilla's "resident welder, grain nerd, and soil whisperer."

In fact, in all the years we did business together, I never saw him cleaned up. He seemed to wear farm dirt like a perfectly natural second skin.

Soon after our singularly unsophisticated debut, Christopher's Table began offering wondrous sandwiches and salads featuring some of the most amazingly fresh produce I have ever tasted. (And not just me. I took some home, and my husband was delighted to find that this stuff stayed fresh in the fridge for 10 days, no wilting—far longer than any grocery store product. Also, Bob—a tough critic—declared these the most flavorful greens he'd ever tasted.) From Noah, I procured a heavenly, ever-morphing mélange of greens: arugula, red leaf, spicy mustard, frisée, and more. It was Noah who first introduced me to garlic scapes, the tender stem and flower bud that grows from a hardneck garlic plant. Garlic scape pesto—*delish*.

Every visit from Noah was a culinary delight. And a personal joy. Noah always arrived with a smile, dropping his remarkable cargo on my counter and usually requesting one of my freshly made sandwiches. On many occasions, he'd barter for additional sandwiches, treasures to share with his farm crew. It was farm to table and back to farm!

It was natural, in more ways than one, to connect with Marini Farm as well, a three-generation fixture atop a hill in the middle of Ipswich, barely two miles west of Christopher's Table.

Michael Marini, Ipswich's native son, was a strapping young farmer, heir apparent to his beloved father, Mario—who still, in his late eighties, can be seen operating a tractor with seemingly endless verve. Mike has become an icon himself over the years, endlessly experimenting with farming techniques, yet always pursuing the priority of providing fresh, safe food for local customers. One ground rule he established for Marini Farm: only plant your own seeds. A few years ago, when other outlets on the North Shore saw much of their produce ruined by a nasty virus after they planted seeds purchased elsewhere, Marini Farm was able to continue offering a seamless supply of safe, healthy vegetables grown from the farm's own seeds. Mike's ultimate goal is to sell 100 percent of the farm's produce through their own farm stand. (At this writing, their best year so far has come deliciously close, at a stellar 99 percent.) Among Mike's many successful innovations is the hugely popular annual Marini corn maze, an entire field of corn set aside for playing.

Left to right: *Me with Mario and Mike Marini at the Dinner on the Farm event at Marini Farm in Ipswich, MA*

He laughs as he recalls telling his venerable father that he intended to plant an entire field of corn and *not harvest it*. But father Mario has always been eager to try new things. He just smiled and waved his son on, enjoying the adventure.

One might look at Mike and me and puzzle over our partnership. In many ways, we were quite dissimilar—and our work schedules were almost completely opposite, so we rarely, if ever, socialized. But we understood each other: we were fellow business owners, both raising young children, and both in the food business. As the dream of Dinner on the Farm began to come together in my mind, it only made sense to reach out to Mike. He was producing tons of fresh food—and he had *land*.

Sitting in Mike's dining room on Linebrook Road, I pitched the beginnings of my idea for an initial Dinner on the Farm event, and within minutes he was urging me to jump into the passenger seat of his truck for a drive out into the far reaches of his property. Soon we were standing in a vast open field—and in that moment, I could see it all before me. This was the perfect setting.

Mike was an ideal collaborator for such an adventure. He was a dreamer, endlessly optimistic (sometimes barely corralled by his more business-minded wife, Kim). And Mike was exuberant in his love of fresh food. He once walked me out into one of his sprawling cornfields, pulled a fresh ear off its stalk, and handed it to me.

I hesitated.

He clearly expected me to eat it.

"But it's not cooked!" I blurted sheepishly.

Mike roared with laughter—and sank his teeth into an ear of his own.

"It's so frickin' sweet!" he exclaimed, his mouth full of corn. "You're gonna love it!"

He wiped his face with the back of his hand and flashed me his dazzling smile.

So there we stood, two guys in the middle of a farm field, munching fresh corn on the cob, and talking about our common joy: *food*.

Marini Farm became the one and only venue for this glorious experiment. It was known as Dinner on the Farm . . . but it probably couldn't have happened if it wasn't Dinner on *Marini* Farm.

I knew most of my customers well, so it was intriguing to meet newcomers. Especially Luca.

He and his wife, a strikingly beautiful couple, showed up for an event. I greeted them, introduced myself, thanked them for coming. Then Luca opened his mouth to speak—and the words rolled off his tongue with the most intoxicating Italian accent I had ever heard.

I confess, I may have swooned.

Luca was a dark-haired, broad-chested gentleman with piercing eyes, dressed in an understated European style. I can't recall the specifics of our first conversation, but I imagine it as a Charlie Brown cartoon, where the adult speaks gibberish. It wasn't until I heard Luca say "I make cheese for a living" that I snapped out of the siren's spell.

A cheese maker?

Over time, my ability to communicate improved. His sexy Italian cheese maker persona was eventually eclipsed by the taste of his homemade caciocavallo and scamorza.

Luca was the kind of person who was always working on a new project. He had a natural presence. People were drawn to him, and

Me with Luca Mignogna at the Dinner on the Farm event at Marini Farm in Ipswich, MA

listened to him, and trusted him, and wanted to be with him, and wanted to help him succeed. It was *glamour*.

We became friends. Luca had rented a fabulous house in the middle of a working farm. He was making Italian cheese—but doing it in the nearby town of Rowley, a town not known for artisan cheeses.

Yet his cheese was delectable.

Eventually, we decided to take our relationship to the next level. Luca moved in.

Well, he moved his business into Christopher's Table.

In my store, he set up a cheese case, augmenting our offerings of gourmet food. So for a time, we had the dazzle of featuring a huge selection of fabulous locally crafted cheeses.

Those were exotic days, in their own way. (Thanks to Luca, I was briefly introduced to the Vatican's personal mozzarella maker and cheesemonger. Who knew that cheese could get so weird?) But for me and Luca, it wasn't exactly a marriage. Staffing issues ended the cheese adventure. Luca couldn't be there every day in person, and the teenagers I'd hired to sell sandwiches couldn't help customers wanting information about fancy cheeses.

Eventually, the cheese case went away. But what an adventure it was! Luca and I parted ways, but we'll always have the cheese.

When you run a small business, you reach out where you can. You ricochet from one contact to the next, hoping that somehow in this zigzag, pinball world you can make a successful connection.

Enter Andrew, a mischievously roguish descendant of the Cabot family, part of the elite Boston Brahmin set. During the War of 1812, the early Cabots furnished more privateers than any other Massachusetts family. So it seems only fitting that Andrew would arrive in Ipswich to open a distillery named Privateer Rum.

Andrew and I met across the counter of Christopher's Table as he and his crew began routinely arriving for lunch. He invited me to the distillery one afternoon to taste the latest batch of his barrel-aged rum. We came from completely different worlds, but we shared enough common ground to forge a friendship. Months later, he would invite me to a wild after-hours party in the distillery warehouse—complete with a band, posh catering, and secluded, curtained-off rooms with couches and mood lighting. So our relationship, shall we say, solidified. This was a very, very interesting fellow businessperson in the small world of Ipswich, Massachusetts.

We were "beer and wine only"—no full liquor license—so there wasn't a direct connection between Christopher's Table and Andrew's superior aged rum. But Andrew supplied me with some of his rum's extraordinary ingredients—like ultrapure sugar cane and real boiled brown sugar and molasses, some of the most flavorful I've ever tasted. I put Andrew's ingredients to work in our menu, and they took my chocolate chip cookies to a whole new level.

The cast list of fascinating local food-centric celebrities goes on and on. Miranda Russell, of Russell Orchards, a family-owned-and-operated 120-acre fruit farm on the road to the beach. Miranda and Doug, the second generation of Russells to farm the land, learned the business from Doug's father, Max, who had farmed it for thirty years. While most North Shore residents know Miranda as a talented singer, my connection was all about her fabulous fruit!

I connected with Rob Martin, then of Ipswich Ale. Chrissi Pappas at Ipswich Shellfish, a coterie of local clammers and fishermen. Tendercrop Farm, in nearby Newbury, offering organically raised meat. I could fill a book just with features on the wonderful purveyors of fascinating foodstuffs that I encountered, partnered with, and featured at Christopher's Table.

And it all came gloriously together at Dinner on the Farm.

Combine all the production values of a rustic farm wedding with a five-course meal, live music, a tractor-pulled wagon to shuttle guests to the location, and 150 joyous, hungry, delighted people. Together on that opening night, we celebrated local food and drink, and local relationships, on a picture-perfect warm summer evening in June.

We set up two ultralong tables under a tent, with a separate kitchen for the crew. The so-called kitchen was really just another, smaller tent staffed by a gracious family who agreed to work the event—Jeff and Karen Gold and their three boys. The Golds had owned a sporting goods store in downtown Ipswich. Their first and second sons, Jeremy and Nick, worked at various times at Christopher's Table, either in the kitchen or waiting on customers behind the counter. For Dinner on the Farm, however, it was all hands on deck.

Dad Jeff tended bar for us, assisted by son Jeremy's girlfriend.

Jeremy provided music, playing with his band. (Years later, Jeremy would go on to make quite a name for himself in the Nashville music industry, hanging out and working with the likes of Blake Shelton and Kelly Clarkson. Ah yes, I knew him when.)

Mom Karen served as point person for the crew, operating a walkie-talkie at the bottom of the hill, managing transportation. Yes, transportation. We had to run a shuttle from down on Linebrook Road because nobody could climb that hill—or even if they could, who would want to?

Youngest son Andrew was also pressed into service—and he was not happy about his assignment: he sat on a milk crate in the

My parents, Frank and Janet DeStefano, along with other guests, travel by tractor-pulled wagon to the Dinner on the Farm event at Marini Farm in Ipswich, MA

middle of a field with a garden hose, washing dishes. (Andrew, boy, I owe ya.)

For three years in a row, we staged a Dinner on the Farm. These became some of my most treasured memories, and greatly cherished by the hundreds who attended.

And if there was an individual who truly made Dinner on the Farm possible, it was Peter. My superb sous-chef. The one person who truly made it possible for this extraordinary experience to occur.

Even *thinking* about doing farm dinners was impossible after Peter was gone.

Andrew Gold, the youngest of the Gold clan, pressed into service as a "dishwasher" at the Dinner on the Farm event at Marini Farm in Ipswich, MA

Blackberry and Thyme Margarita

When guests arrived at Marini Farm for our Dinner on the Farm event, they were greeted with this refreshing cocktail as they waited to be transported to the dinner site by hay wagon.

1 (6-ounce) package fresh blackberries, divided
4 small fresh thyme sprigs, divided
4 ounces premium silver tequila
¼ cup simple syrup
3 tablespoons fresh lime juice
1 ounce Cointreau or other orange liqueur
2 cups ice cubes, divided
Chilled sparkling water

Makes 2 servings

Set aside 4 blackberries to be used as a garnish. Put the remaining blackberries and 2 thyme sprigs in a medium bowl. Mash the solids with a muddler or the back of a wooden spoon.

Mix in the tequila, simple syrup, lime juice, and Cointreau, then 1 cup of the ice. Stir to blend well.

Divide the remaining 1 cup of ice between two rocks glasses.

Strain the margarita mixture over the ice in each glass. Top with sparkling water. Garnish each with 2 of the reserved blackberries and 1 thyme sprig.

Farmhouse Gazpacho

Talk about a home run recipe! This cold soup is not only delicious and refreshing on a hot day but also a great way to use up all those summer garden vegetables. I still remember filling five gallon buckets with this soup to be used as a first course for our farm dinners.

1 hothouse cucumber, halved and seeded but not peeled
2 red peppers, cored and seeded
1 yellow pepper, cored and seeded
4 plum tomatoes
1 red onion
3 garlic cloves, minced
3 cups tomato juice (not V8)
¼ cup white vinegar
¼ cup good olive oil
1½ teaspoons kosher salt
1 teaspoon pepper

Makes 6 servings

Chop the cucumber, red peppers, yellow pepper, tomatoes, and onion into 1- to 2-inch pieces.

Put each vegetable separately into a food processor fitted with a steel blade and pulse until coarsely chopped. (I prefer my gazpacho to have texture and be chunky, so I do not puree it.)

Combine the vegetables in a large bowl. Add the garlic, tomato juice, vinegar, olive oil, salt, and pepper. Mix well and chill before serving. Once the gazpacho is properly chilled, it will be ready to eat—however, the longer it sits, the more flavorful it will become.

Watermelon Salad with Feta

When you have over a hundred people sitting in a farm field in the middle of summer, you have to serve things that will help people beat the heat. The watermelon in this fun salad is so refreshing and pairs perfectly with the tangy feta cheese.

Dressing:
2 tablespoons extra-virgin olive oil
3 tablespoons lime juice
½ garlic clove, minced
¼ teaspoon sea salt

Salad:
2 cups mixed greens
1 heaping cup diced English cucumber
¼ cup thinly sliced red onions
1 cup cherry tomatoes, halved
5 cups cubed, seeded watermelon
⅓ cup crumbled feta cheese
⅓ cup torn mint or basil leaves
½ jalapeño or serrano pepper, thinly sliced (optional)

Makes 4 servings

To make the dressing, whisk together the olive oil, lime juice, garlic, and salt in a small bowl.

In a separate bowl, combine the mixed greens, cucumber, red onion, and cherry tomatoes.

Arrange the watermelon on a plate and drizzle with half the dressing. Place the salad greens mixture on top of the watermelon. Top with feta, mint, and serrano pepper and drizzle with the remaining dressing. Season to taste with sea salt and pepper and serve.

Note: For the Dinner on the Farm event, we cut the watermelon into 4 x 2-inch rounds instead of cubes and topped them with the salad mix for a special presentation. Do what works best for you.

Roasted Vegetable Tart with Goat Cheese Custard

The menus at our Dinner on the Farm events always indicated the distance the ingredients traveled for each course. The ingredients for this tart were so local that the distance was less than one mile!

Pastry:
- 8 tablespoons unsalted butter, chilled and diced
- 1¾ cups flour
- 1 egg yolk
- 1 teaspoon salt

Filling:
- 1 yellow summer squash, sliced into ½-inch circles
- 1 zucchini, sliced into ½-inch circles
- 1 red pepper, sliced into thin rings
- 1 cup fresh corn
- 1 tablespoon olive oil
- 2 eggs, beaten
- 1½ tablespoons whole milk
- 1 tablespoon thyme leaves
- 1 teaspoon sea salt
- 1 teaspoon pepper
- 2 ounces soft goat cheese
- 2½ tablespoons pine nuts

Makes 6–8 servings

To make the pastry, pulse the butter and flour in a food processor until the mixture resembles fine crumbs.

Add the egg yolk, salt, and 1 teaspoon water and pulse until the mixture forms a dough. Dump the dough onto a lightly floured surface, shape it into a ball, cover it in plastic wrap, and then refrigerate it while you make the filling.

Preheat the oven to 400°F.

For the filling, toss the squash, zucchini, red pepper, and corn with the olive oil and spread it on a baking sheet. Roast for 20 minutes or until the vegetables are tender and browned in spots.

Lightly flour your work surface and roll out the chilled dough until it is ½ inch thick and wide enough to fill a 10-inch tart pan. Place the dough in the tart pan with some overhang, then trim the edges to neaten. Refrigerate for 10 minutes.

Transfer the chilled tart pan onto a sheet pan and bake for 12 minutes. If the dough bubbles up, gently pierce it with a fork.

Reduce the oven temperature to 350°F.

Spread the vegetable mixture into the parbaked crust.

In a separate bowl, mix the eggs, milk, thyme, salt, and pepper. Pour the mixture over the vegetables.

Crumble the goat cheese over the top, sprinkle with pine nuts, and bake for 12 to 14 minutes, until the cheese is golden, the pine nuts have taken on a little color, and the filling is hot. Remove from the oven and serve warm.

Grilled Flank Steak with Blistered Vegetables and Herbs

Feeding 150 people in a field, on a farm, without a stove or oven was terrifying, but this beautiful main course was a breeze to execute simply by firing up the grill.

Steak:
- ⅔ cup olive oil
- ½ cup balsamic vinegar
- 4 cloves garlic, finely chopped
- 2 teaspoons kosher salt
- 1 teaspoon pepper
- 5 to 6 fresh thyme sprigs
- 1 (3-pound) piece flank steak (or skirt steak)

Vegetables:
- 1 tablespoon olive oil
- 2 large shallots, sliced
- 3 cloves garlic, sliced
- 1 pint heirloom cherry tomatoes (I prefer multicolored)

Basil vinaigrette:
- 1 shallot, roughly chopped
- 2 cups tightly packed fresh basil leaves
- 1 clove garlic, peeled
- ½ teaspoon red pepper flakes
- ½ cup olive oil
- 2 tablespoons red wine vinegar
- 1 teaspoon kosher salt

Makes 4 servings

To make the marinade, whisk together the oil, vinegar, garlic, salt, and pepper in a large bowl. Add the thyme.

Add the steak to the bowl and flip to coat. Cover with plastic wrap and refrigerate for at least 8 hours and up to 24 hours.

For the charred vegetables, heat the oil in a heavy cast-iron skillet over medium-high heat. Add the shallot and garlic and cook for 1 minute, or until fragrant.

Add the cherry tomatoes and cook without stirring for 2 minutes, or until they start to blister. Stir quickly, turn off the heat, and let them sit for another 2 minutes or so. Season with salt and pepper.

For the basil vinaigrette, blend the shallot, basil, garlic, red pepper flakes, oil, vinegar, and salt in a blender for 1 to 2 minutes, until very smooth. Season with more salt and pepper. This dressing will keep in an airtight container refrigerated for up to 3 days.

Preheat an outdoor grill or grill pan to medium-high heat and oil the grates. Remove the steak from the marinade, letting the excess drip off. Season liberally with salt and pepper.

Grill the steak, turning occasionally, until lightly charred all over, 10 to 12 minutes for medium.

Transfer the steak to a cutting board and let it rest for 5 to 10 minutes.

To serve, thinly slice the steak against the grain and drizzle with the basil vinaigrette and top with the charred tomatoes. Serve extra vinaigrette on the side.

Grilled Peaches with Mascarpone Cream and Crumbled Amaretti

This is a simple and elegant dessert, but make sure to use freestone peaches—you can just slice the peach down the middle and pull it right off the pit. They're available mid-June to mid-August.

Whipped mascarpone:
1 cup heavy cream
¼ cup confectioners' sugar
½ cup mascarpone
2 tablespoons amaretto liqueur

Peaches:
½ cup sugar
2 teaspoons pure vanilla extract
4 strips lemon zest
¼ cup lemon juice
¼ cup amaretto liqueur
½ cup water
4 medium peaches, halved and pitted
1 tablespoon canola oil
2 ounces amaretti cookies, crushed

Makes 4 servings

To make the whipped mascarpone, in the bowl of a stand mixer fitted with a whisk attachment, beat the heavy cream and confectioners' sugar on high speed until soft peaks form. Add the mascarpone and amaretto liqueur and beat until well combined. Transfer the resulting cream to a serving bowl and refrigerate until ready to serve.

To make the syrup, put the sugar, vanilla, lemon zest, lemon juice, amaretto, and water in a small saucepan. Bring to a boil over medium-high heat. Reduce the heat to medium and let simmer for 10 minutes, until sugar is dissolved. Remove the pan from the heat and let cool to room temperature, about 30 minutes.

Place the peaches in a large baking dish and pour the syrup over them. Let the peaches soak in the syrup for 1 hour, turning them halfway through.

Heat a grill to medium-high. Brush the grill pan with canola oil. Reduce the heat to medium. Remove the peaches from the syrup, reserving the syrup for serving. Place the peaches cut side down on the grill and cook undisturbed until grill marks appear, 4 to 5 minutes. Flip the peaches and grill until the skins are charred and the fruit is soft, 4 to 5 minutes more.

Remove the peaches from the grill. Serve with whipped mascarpone and crumbled amaretti cookies.

PART IV

THE GOOD KID

What Do You Want to Do?

"He's a good kid."

It wasn't the first time a parent came to ask me if I could hire their child.

"He just needs to find something he's good at."

I had always liked this woman. She'd been a Christopher's Table customer for a year or so. A successful Ipswich business owner. Confident. Fearless, even.

But that morning, I thought I sensed a bit of anxiety in her voice. A mother urgently wanting to help her son.

Peter arrived for his first day of work, not quite twenty years of age, tall and lanky, somewhat guarded. A good-looking, serious face with piercing blue eyes. But it seemed to me there might be a million secrets hidden behind them. Or maybe this is simply a mystery I imagine now, retroactively, all these years later.

It wasn't a formal interview, but Peter presented himself well. His answers were honest and articulate. The emerging facts, however, were quite straightforward: Do you cook? *Yes.* Any experience in a professional kitchen? *No.* Do you cook at home? *Yes.* What are you looking for? *I'm really looking for something to do; I need to make a little money; I'm a hard worker.* (All good answers.) Do you want to cook? Wash dishes? What do you want to do? What do you enjoy? How much work do you want?

He didn't have any substantial experience that I could automatically make use of, but there was something about him, something that told me he was intelligent and ready. He wasn't like other "kids" who had come my way looking for work—kids who signaled, *This one's gonna take a lot of effort.* Peter was different. And I knew his mother. He came from a reputable family. Frankly, that counted for something.

And I always wanted to help people. If my little store could help somebody, I considered that a win. Plus, I could use an extra pair of hands.

We began immediately: he showed up the next day. I'd just have him do some basic stuff and see how it went, see if he liked it.

He did like it. I did too.

On day one, I laid out a couple of recipes—simple stuff. "We're gonna make chicken salad." I put the recipe in front of him. "You're gonna roast. That means you're gonna season the chicken, you're gonna put the chicken in the oven. If you have questions, you're gonna ask me while the chicken is cooking. You're gonna dice celery and grapes and walnuts. Then we're gonna chop and shred the chicken." I just wanted to see how he worked. How he held a knife. Did he obsess over slicing celery, or did he just do it?

Over the next days and weeks, I found Peter to be a bit reserved but polite, bright, and eager to learn. Maybe most important of all, he was a natural in the kitchen. He was unafraid. Determined to learn. If he made a mistake, he didn't freak out. He simply dug in and set out to try again. Not something I observed in many people his age. Many's the young kitchen assistant who would hold the celery like it's a snake, or make a single cut and beg for direction: Is this all right? Should I keep going? I was looking for a tone of confidence. Peter was confident. If he didn't get it exactly right—if I said, "You don't need to cut it so small, you can keep the pieces bigger"—he'd nod and try again. There was no "Oh shit, I screwed up!" Peter took direction and correction, and he was fine with it all.

Over time, Peter's initial—what shall I call it?—*reserve* relaxed. He seemed to lower his guard. We got along well, despite our age difference. We came to enjoy conversations about food, politics, movies. It was never like talking to "a teenager." He was mature. We had substantial conversations. We came to be two guys working side by side in the kitchen. We laughed at vulgar jokes. We turned up the radio when we heard a favorite song. We played pranks on one another (a typical restaurant kitchen routine).

He was just part time when he started, but he became a valuable asset. I came to rely on him in ways you wouldn't expect from an inexperienced walk-in-off-the-street employee. It didn't happen overnight, but he learned easily. He could follow a recipe, and he took initiative—and before long, I felt very comfortable saying, "Hey, I have to pick up my kid at preschool. Can you hold down the fort? Can you wait on customers?"

The customers loved Peter too. Hope Wigglesworth, an Ipswich icon (whom we lost in 2017 at the age of ninety), was one of my favorite frequent visitors at Christopher's Table; when Peter arrived, he and Hope hit it off immediately. Peter was unfazed by her advanced age and polished upper-class breeding. In turn, Hope never flinched at Peter's youth and spoke with him at great length on a variety of topics. Peter was delighted even by Hope's historic family name. "Her name makes her sound like a Muppet!" he laughed. Hope, who had a great sense of humor, would have loved this—and perhaps loves it even now.

Peter came to be a Christopher's Table rock star. He had all the pieces you want: personality, brains, work ethic, easy to get along with. Well rounded! I salute his parents, because both Peter and his sister, Claudia, were exemplary human beings.

Eventually, Peter shared more about his personal issues. He had struggled with substances, though he was clean when he arrived at my door, and he had dealt with depression. But these are not foreign or taboo issues in a professional kitchen; over the years, I had worked with many, many people who could have told me similar stories.

And Peter consistently did very well. There were some really exceptional moments where I realized I was watching him grow as a young man and an outstanding worker.

No, I never harbored a secret desire for Peter to become a professional chef. He never indicated that he wanted to be. But I have no doubt Peter could have excelled in a number of professions. He was just *that person*.

One Friday afternoon, when my son Alex was perhaps six years old, Peter arrived at work with a big plastic bag filled with video game cartridges and an old handheld PlayStation device.

"I don't use this anymore," he said. "Maybe Alex will enjoy it?"

The answer was yes. (Alex, nineteen years old as I write these words, still has all that PlayStation gear!) It was a kind gesture, a side of Peter I was seeing more and more. Later that day, Peter had a lot of questions about my kids. How Bob and I had decided to adopt our two boys. What the process looked like. What it meant to be a dad. I'd heard from Peter about his girlfriend, Jenna. I understood they weren't quite ready to settle down, but it was clear that he had designs on starting a family, maybe even being a dad himself one day.

Peter never knew what a blessing he was. Whenever people casually asked me about "how wonderful it is" to be a business owner, working for myself, I always came back to a kind of seesaw: loving the freedom and the independence—but also feeling the burden—something I never foresaw—of *loneliness*. When you're the only person in charge of a small prepared-food shop, every decision you have to make, every problem you have to solve, even every victory you have to celebrate, you do by yourself. No colleagues to share it with. No supervisors to consult. No partners to collaborate with. I often felt isolated. Peter changed the equation. He was "only" my twenty-year-old employee, but I could run ideas by him, ask his opinions. His presence in my kitchen made me feel less alone. To me, in that world, this was huge. He took on more and more responsibility. *Peter's closing up. Peter's getting everything ready for tomorrow. This or that is in the fridge? No problem. Peter's on it.*

Before Peter had worked with me in the kitchen for a year, I promoted him to sous-chef and gave him a raise. The promotion was earned and well deserved. He was taking on more and more work. He could handle independent projects and always completed them reliably. I came to rely on Peter in ways that gave me opportunities to step away from the kitchen and handle other matters. Eventually, I found that I could leave early, see more of my family. Peter was solid in his role; he knew my recipes inside and out and executed them flawlessly. Perhaps the greatest gift Peter gave me was the ability to take an afternoon off and spend more time with my children.

I attended the annual Fancy Food Show every summer, which showcased the kind of new products I liked to offer at Christopher's Table. In the exhibition hall at this massive convention, you'd find some awesome new pita chips, fabulous new hummus, astounding new chocolate bars, whatever—sort of a real-life Willy Wonka experience. One year, when profits were strong, I took Peter with me, and we had a great time.

But I sensed, during that trip, that Peter was dealing with issues under the surface, issues that I didn't and couldn't fully understand.

We were working in the kitchen one afternoon, Peter making marinade for our steak tips, me chopping grapes and celery for our chicken salad.

"Hey, boss, can I ask you a question?" Peter began, strangely hesitant. "Actually, it's more of a favor."

I looked up from my work and waited.

"I turn twenty-one this month," Peter said, "and I was wondering . . . I was curious if you might . . . if you'd be willing to go out and celebrate with me."

I was gobsmacked. For what felt like a long time, I stood there silently. Finally I was able to speak: "Why would you want to celebrate such a milestone with *me*? I'm old enough to be—well, to be your cool gay uncle!"

Peter laughed. Then he proceeded to explain that he didn't put much stock into turning twenty-one and had no interest in going out for a night of excessive drinking; he was really looking for something more low key. Then he offered his idea: maybe we could go to a *strip club*.

"I wouldn't exactly call that 'low key'!" I snorted.

But I quickly recovered, channeling the cool gay uncle vibe, and suggested that we could go see a drag show in Boston. Peter's face lit up—a kid at Christmas. "That would be incredible!"

On a Saturday evening we made our way through the dimly lit side streets of Boston's Bay Village neighborhood. I pointed to an unassuming brick building on the corner. "This is it," I told him. We'd arrived at Jacques Cabaret, Boston's longest-operating gay bar, launched in 1938 and hosting weekly drag performances ever since. Inside, in the front room, a rough-looking crowd of blue-collar type guys were gathered at the bar and around a pool table. Transexuals in high heels and short skirts flirted their way around the bar, soliciting cocktails from interested gentlemen.

I could see the confusion and bewilderment on Peter's face as he took it all in. "I'll explain later," I whispered, and ushered him through the crowd and around the bar to the small stage and cabaret-style seating where the performance would take place. Inside me, a pang of guilt rose; I wondered if this was all too much for my young friend. But before I could ask, Peter was making a beeline for a small table right next to the stage.

"Let's sit up front so we don't miss anything!" he shouted over his shoulder. As we took our seats, I tried to explain the possible ramifications of sitting so close to the stage: we'd be prime targets for the performers' antics. "Drag queens can be a bit lecherous to guys in the audience," I advised. "Especially straight guys." Peter shared none of my concern. He could hardly wait for the show to start!

If I hadn't known better, I'd have thought Peter was an old hand at all this. We sat sipping overpriced watered-down drinks as various tried-and-true celebrity look-alikes lip-synched their way across the stage: Britney Spears, Dolly Parton, Eartha Kitt, and others.

Everything was going smoothly until Peter unwittingly caught the attention of the show's emcee, an oversized and over-the-top queen by the name of Kris Knievel. Suddenly—so quickly that I had no time to object or intervene—Peter was being pulled out of his seat and onto center stage. With the intensity of a pit bull sizing up a pork chop, Ms. Knievel began peppering Peter with raunchy questions, overt sexual advances, and even a request for a spotlight to accentuate Peter's "assets." The audience roared, and kept roaring, for more.

I, on the other hand, was sitting there in utter panic. I was responsible! I felt it was my job to protect this kid and keep him safe.

I didn't think the situation could get any worse until Peter shouted from the stage, "Hey, boss, hold my shirt!" As the music surged to a speaker-shaking decibel level, Peter flung me his T-shirt and began to dance bare chested around the stage. The audience went ballistic as Peter and Ms. Knievel gyrated, grinding to the throbbing beat.

No, not exactly low key. Nor traditional. Not even rational. But this is how we celebrated Peter's twenty-first birthday. Exactly as he wanted it!

Months passed; good times. But then, abruptly, Peter gave me two weeks' notice.

He was engaged to Jenna. They were ecstatic about it. Looking ahead, Peter said, he needed to make more money. But no, he didn't have another job lined up.

My right-hand man, Peter Bowman, at the Dinner on the Farm event at Marini Farm in Ipswich, MA

I put on my dad hat. Life lesson: you don't quit one job until you have another one lined up.

Peter wasn't hearing it. After two awkward weeks, he left. I wished him well. We hugged. And he was gone.

Perhaps a month or two later, he showed up at Christopher's Table with his fiancée. "What's up, boss? Just came to say hello." It was great to see him. We parted warmly.

I have come to realize he wasn't really saying hello. He was saying goodbye.

A week later, on a rainy school-day morning, I watched my boys get on the school bus. I was still at the end of my driveway when my cell phone rang. The voice was unfamiliar. The message was impossible.

A friend of Peter's family was calling to let me know: Peter—my dear Peter—was gone. He had taken his own life. Overdosed, in the bathtub, all alone.

My knees buckled, my heart began racing, my hands were shaking. It didn't make sense.

It still doesn't. I had so many questions. I still do.

I love remembering Peter's twenty-first birthday because he was free, unencumbered, even if only for the briefest of moments. He embraced joy that night. I imagine he didn't get to do that very often. I am grateful I had the privilege of experiencing that crazy, joyous evening with him.

In the end, the burden Peter carried, whatever it may have been, became too much for him to carry.

I feel fortunate for Peter's time in my life. He will always be a cherished part of the Christopher's Table legacy. I'm grateful that he was someone I could call my friend.

Yet Peter's death left a gaping hole in my heart. Perhaps the wound has grown smaller with each passing year, but I suspect it will never fully close.

I truly could not imagine doing another Dinner on the Farm without my bright, beloved right-hand man.

And I didn't.

An evening event at Christopher's Table meant we, in the kitchen, needed something to eat, so Peter developed a habit of making us chicken cordon bleu. But he liked to swap out Swiss cheese and swap in cheddar. And then he liked to pour ranch dressing all over it. He proudly christened this new concoction Chicken Cordon Peter. I confess, it was yummy.

But then he began nudging me about it. "Put this in the case; let's sell it." He wanted Chicken Cordon Peter to be "official" at Christopher's Table.

Uh no, Peter, sorry.

Until now. I'm finally, with no small measure of guilt, including the recipe in this cookbook. I loved it. Now you can too. If Peter is reading this, somewhere in the universe, he's smiling.

Peter lives on.

Peter and me testing recipes for the Dinner on the Farm event in the kitchen at Christopher's Table in Ipswich, MA

Chicken Cordon Peter

Peter was my sous-chef at Christopher's Table, and he would always make this adaptation of chicken cordon bleu for us to eat while we were working. Don't forget the ranch dressing!

2 chicken breast cutlets
2 eggs, lightly beaten
1 cup seasoned bread crumbs
Canola oil for frying
4 slices deli ham
4 slices cheddar cheese, or ½ cup shredded
Ranch dressing

Makes 2 servings

Preheat the oven to 350°F.

Season the chicken breast cutlets with salt and pepper. Place them in the eggs and turn to coat. Dredge the cutlets through the seasoned breadcrumbs.

In a large frying pan, heat 4 to 5 tablespoons of oil until shimmering but not smoking. Fry the cutlets until golden brown and cooked through, 4 to 5 minutes per side.

Place the chicken cutlets on a sheet pan. Top each cutlet with two slices of ham and two slices of cheddar.

Put the sheet pan in the oven until the cheese is melted.

Serve with generous amounts of ranch dressing, just as Peter would.

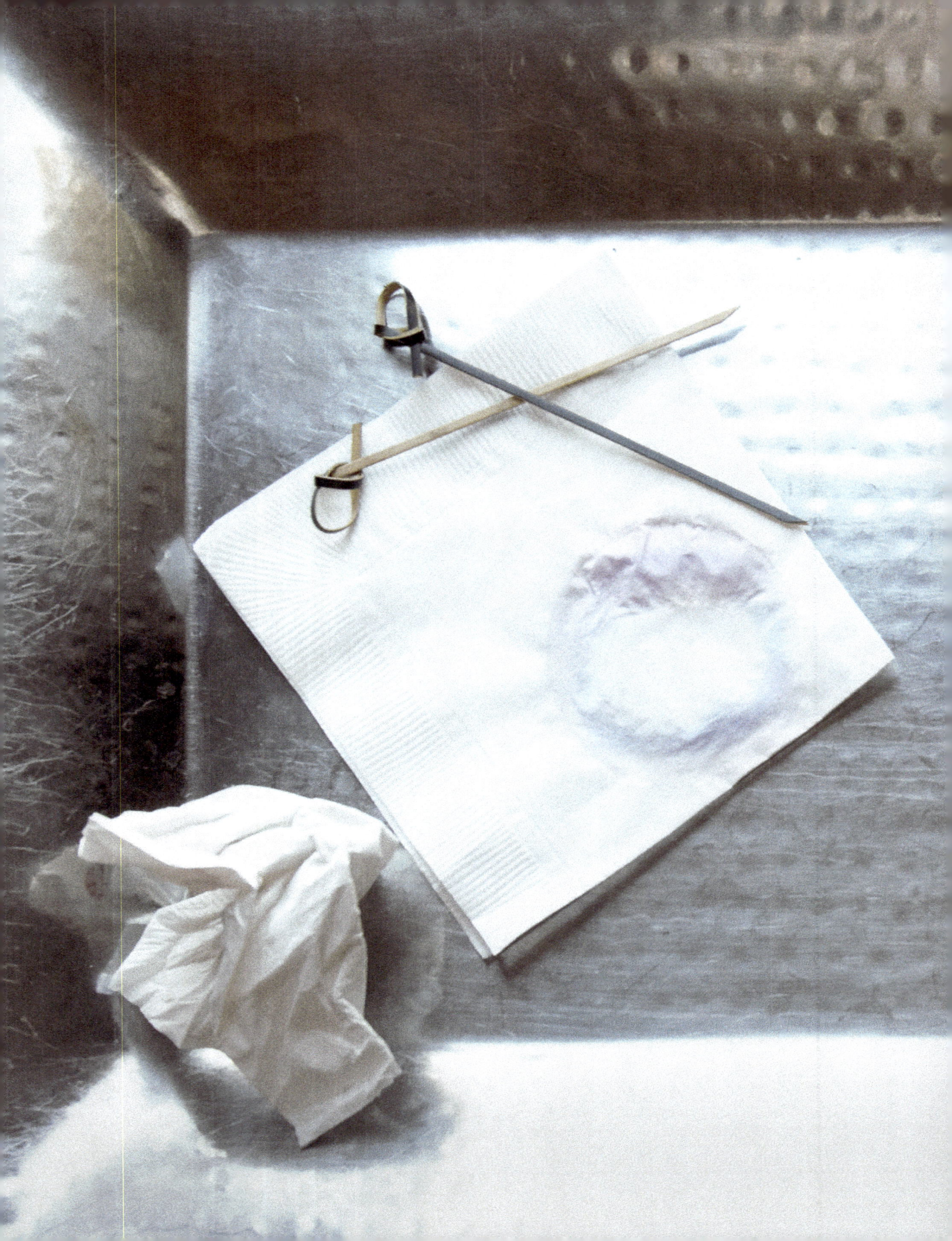

PART V

FIRE AND FRIENDSHIP

The Martha Stewart Moment

I came home from a catering job and called my mother in tears.

"Oh my God," she said, "what's wrong?"

"I was catering a job," I cried, "and the house caught on fire and burned to the ground."

"Jesus Christ, Christopher," she replied. "What did you do!?"

"Nothing!" I replied. "Mom, I didn't do anything! I didn't cause the fire!"

I have worked in catering forever. For many in the restaurant industry, catering is a lifeline, the single most lucrative work, hour for hour, and often the most consistent work available. In a prepared-food shop, you sell a sandwich or two at a time, a cup or bowl of soup at a time, maybe a pound of chicken salad. Let's face it: even full eight-hour days in the shop weren't producing record-breaking revenues. But catering a celebration of life for fifty people in tony Beverly Farms meant driving home with a big, fat check in my pocket, a sum that likely rivaled three eight-hour days at the shop. Of course, some in the food biz want to spend their lives just catering. But that wasn't me. My little local shop was my dream, my vision, my passion. I loved the sound of the bell above the door signaling the arrival of another customer. "Good morning, Mrs. Kostopoulos! How are you?" You don't get that with catering. There's no love in catering. It's a volume business; it's paying the bills. There's nothing sexy about mashed potatoes for eighty people. My little Christopher's Table storefront afforded me the luxury of leaning on the cash register and drinking coffee and chatting with a neighbor, a customer, a vendor on the other side of the counter.

My husband says I am always trying to have "Martha Stewart moments": seeing something—some perfect scenario with perfect people in some perfect situation—imagining myself in the picture, and refusing to give up the vision until I can re-create it in real life. Maybe Bob's right. I certainly did envision Christopher's Table. I wanted a prepared-food shop because I wanted to open it up in the morning, all alone, with sunlight streaming in through the window, and make a pot of coffee, and bake muffins, or scones, or maybe cupcakes. None of the intense pressure of a restaurant kitchen: 120 people ordering dinner at the same time and the sous-chef just cut off his pinky, someone's overdosing in the walk-in, and the medium-rare steak was sent back for being too pink. Others can thrive on that. I'm a misfit in that picture. The little neighborhood shop is *my* picture. *Look at these little quiches I made!* That's the Martha Stewart moment; that's the world I love.

My Martha Stewart moments aren't limited to food. When our boys were still quite young, I envisioned the perfect Christmas card photo, shot in a bucolic wildlife sanctuary in neighboring Topsfield. I booked the magical local photographer Cynthia August, and Bob and I schlepped the boys out there in their perfect outfits with their perfect haircuts. Cynthia cleverly brought birdseed; birds gathered and ate out of the boys' hands for the most awesome Christmas card photo ever. But the property was all muck and mire, crisscrossed by long, snaking boardwalks. At one point, five-year-old Lucas took off running. Where the boardwalk turned, Lucas didn't. With Cynthia's camera still click-click-clicking, Lucas suddenly disappeared with a *blup!* I've never run so fast in my life. I pulled him from the muddy waters, cold and wet and crying. "I hope you're happy," Bob said. "You succeeded in creating your Martha Stewart moment." Well, what can I say? Yes, it was terrifying for a few seconds, and yes, our son could have drowned, but the Christmas card photo was phenomenal!

There was a day, early on, when I found myself leaning on the counter at Christopher's Table, looking out the front window on a sunny day, holding my coffee mug in that perfect, long-dreamed position. *Okay,* I said to myself, with no small measure of self-satisfaction, *I did it. This is what I wanted.* No, I wasn't getting rich on muffin money. But that didn't matter to me. What mattered was that I'd made it happen. I was happy.

Except that, yeah, it did matter. Muffins weren't paying the bills. Catering was crucial to close the gap.

Catering isn't necessarily a matter of organizing a big staff to deliver a ton of food to a huge event. It can also be a small, personal, *exclusive* service. When I began striving to make my living as a chef—not knowing what the hell I was doing—my first regular client was a family who lived at the Ipswich Country Club. It wasn't "cook and deliver." It was "bring your ingredients and go to their house and good luck" cooking. Day one, I was scared out of my mind. They didn't know it, but I was making it up as I went.

Do you imagine this as glamorous? The gourmet chef commanding the scene, ordering the clients out of the kitchen in order to create the art? Wrong. I arrived midday, while the clients were away at work or the golf course or who knows where. I was given the code to the alarm system; I let myself into the house. I was there with the cleaning people. I worked alone in the kitchen and left my masterpieces in the fridge and let myself out. The gourmet elf.

I have not entirely outgrown this work. To this day, I have a weekly catering client I serve in this way. The client has a severe food allergy and hires me because it's simpler and safer than eating out. I let myself in, I let myself out. The dog waits for me at the door—insisting on serving as my kitchen buddy, or perhaps as a spy from the board of health. The dog never leaves my side, from start to finish. For years, for another client, I actually cooked for the dog. Not the humans. The dog. The glitzy life of a chef? No.

Realtors love the personal chef idea. I routinely sold gift certificates to realtors, which they could present to their clients upon the sale of a house. Congratulations! Enjoy a gourmet meal, cooked in your new home!

At the very beginning of my catering career—when I was still truly clueless—a prominent local realtor bought a gift certificate and gave it to a young couple, not yet married, who had just purchased their first home in Boxford, Massachusetts. So I set off for Boxford to cook dinner for the two homeowners. I showed up in the pouring rain. I prepared dinner for them, uneventfully, and they enjoyed it. Months later, the woman called to ask if I would prepare dinner for their wedding—thirty people.

I was still terribly green, making stuff up as I went along. I didn't have proper catering equipment for a wedding—even one with only thirty guests—no chafing dishes, no plates or glassware, nothing. But I was still working as director of performing arts at Suffolk University, so I went to the school cafeteria and asked the manager to lend me five chafing dishes and some other essentials.

Thus armed, I worked out a fabulous menu with the bride and groom: butternut squash and apple soup, fillet of beef, and on and on. On the big day, I arrived—it was early winter, it was cold, with snow already on the ground, early in the season—with an assistant I'll call Joyce. We were there well ahead of the guests, of course, so there were no cars in the long curved driveway. We pulled up to the two-car garage and unloaded our borrowed gear into the house.

"You're gonna want to move your car to the street," the husband-to-be said, "because the guests will block you in." Wise advice. As the guests arrived, their cars filled the driveway in two long lanes, side by side.

The couple owned two enormous dogs. They loved the dogs, but the dogs were not invited to the wedding. They would be staying in a room downstairs off the garage, while the vows were exchanged in the living room upstairs. My assistant, Joyce, would pass champagne on trays during the ceremony portion of the evening while I continued working on the meal to be served in the dining room afterward.

Joyce was still circulating with a tray of champagne flutes—I was ladling soup, the first course—when the fire alarm went off. I immediately assumed I had erred. *Is the beef tenderloin burning? Was the oven not cleaned properly? What's happening?* But a quick check indicated nothing amiss in the kitchen.

It was soon evident to our friends in the living room that smoke was coursing up from the basement. I heard people calling out, "Everybody out of the house!"

Guests in suits and lovely dresses began dashing out—no coats, no purses, no cell phones; all that stuff was piled up in a bedroom somewhere. I was the only one with a phone who could call 911. It was like the sinking of the *Titanic*: Joyce and I found ourselves shepherding people down the stairs and out the front door. Even though I was only being paid a modest fee to cook beef tenderloin, I somehow became responsible for getting this entire wedding full of people out of the house while it burned.

People stood shivering in the snow, in their wedding attire, still holding their champagne glasses, as flames began licking up through the windows.

The bride stood on the sidewalk screaming—not over the destruction of the house, but at the realization that their two beloved dogs were still in the basement inside. A gasp went up from the crowd as the bride suddenly bolted back into the house. Nobody could stop her.

And she didn't return quickly. People were crying, groaning, yelling. Finally, the bride reappeared—not from the front door, but from the side of the house—with her hands under the dogs' collars as they lurched toward us in terror.

The house went up fast—along with all the wedding gifts; everyone's coats, purses, cell phones, and plane tickets home; and Suffolk University's cafeteria equipment. Everything was gone. And as if to add insult to injury, the guests' cars, jammed together in the driveway two by two, began catching on fire in succession, windows popping from the pressure. Even the latecomers, parked farthest from the flames, couldn't move their cars away because their keys were trapped inside the house, in the inferno.

The Boxford Fire Department couldn't get there quickly enough. The house burned to the foundation. Along with the beef tenderloin.

Much to my chagrin, I was a "person of interest," so I had to go into the fire station and answer questions. But it was quickly determined that the caterer and his assistant were innocent, not responsible for the fire. The culprit turned out to be fuel for a wood-pellet stove, delivered the day before the wedding, stacked in the garage, almost high enough to touch the ceiling. Fire department investigators surmised that the bride or groom pulled their own car into the garage to make room on the driveway for guests, and the nose of the car—still hot—ignited the huge ladderlike pillar of wood pellets. The flames shot upward in seconds, burning the garage ceiling, and soon, above it, the floor of the house's first story.

The bride and groom came away from their wedding day with nothing, not even a toothbrush. They moved in with their parents, and friends pitched in to help them rebuild their lives. Having gone through that traumatic event with them, I felt a special connection as well. I called them frequently and often dropped off food. They remained surprisingly upbeat, despite the tragedy. The bride had a hobby of painting wooden rocking chairs for children in fantastic colors, and she presented one to me for my son Alex, whose adoption had just gone through.

Eventually, determined not to be defeated, and with insurance paying the bills, the couple rebuilt the house on its original foundation. Insurance reimbursed Suffolk for the cafeteria gear too. To celebrate their triumph, the bride and groom threw a big party—I hesitate to call it a "housewarming" party—but they didn't hire me to cater it. Instead, to my delight, I was invited as a guest. I guess friendships really are forged in fire.

Catering in someone's home or place of business, you observe basic protocols, you maintain a certain sense of propriety.

In your own joint, you can do whatever the hell you want.

Events at Christopher's Table could be staid and proper . . . but they were just as likely to qualify as no holds barred.

Like when a prominent Ipswich-based artist, a flamboyant longtime friend I'll call Cindy, brought me an out-of-the-ordinary request. She was approaching a milestone birthday, and she envisioned a party with three essential components: (a) chocolate and (b) champagne, served by (c) handsome men with no shirts on.

Try bringing this idea to your local caterer—I dare you. I loved

Cindy and I loved this idea! But before agreeing to cater this shindig, I made one important stipulation: I would need to lead the auditions—er, interviews—for the hunky shirtless servers. Cindy, who happened to be gifted with a beautiful singing voice, wondered what I thought about her singing a song or two at the party. My response was quick: "It's your party, of course you can perform!" But I had another stipulation. For such an extraordinary event, if she was going to sing for her guests, she would need to make an entrance: four of the burly, half-naked servers would carry Cindy in on a palanquin, Cleopatra-style. If we were going to go through the trouble of finding such willing beefcakes, we might as well put them to good use. No surprise, the ever-theatrical Cindy enthusiastically agreed.

My sous-chef, Peter, began building the palanquin, and I reached out to my friends in the Boston entertainment world. Soon I was sitting in the kitchen of Christopher's Table interviewing beautiful young men, asking them to take off their shirts and hold a tray of champagne glasses. I marveled at the journey from humble little muffin maker to topless-male-model talent agent.

We had loads of blowout events at Christopher's Table over the years, but Cindy's birthday was beyond sensational, a night of unforgettable revelry and joy.

Proving, perhaps, that Martha Stewart moments come in all shapes and sizes.

Herb Salad Spring Rolls

These delicious spring rolls are simple, yet labor intensive—don't let that scare you because once you get the hang of making them, you'll want them all the time! Rice paper rounds can be found in the Asian section of most large grocery stores.

1 (2-ounce) package bean thread (cellophane) noodles
1½ tablespoons rice vinegar
2 large Boston lettuce leaves, washed well and spun dry
8 (8-inch) rice paper rounds plus additional in case some tear
2 tablespoons roasted peanuts, crushed
1 green onion, cut into 2-inch julienne strips
¼ cup finely shredded carrot
⅓ cup thinly sliced purple cabbage
¼ cup fresh basil leaves (preferably Thai basil), washed well and spun dry
¼ cup fresh mint leaves, washed well and spun dry
¼ cup fresh coriander leaves, washed well and spun dry
Spicy Peanut Sauce (recipe follows)

Makes 4 servings

Soak the noodles in a bowl of very hot water for 15 minutes, then drain well in a colander. Reserve half the noodles for another use. With scissors, cut the remaining noodles into 3- to 4-inch lengths. In a small bowl, toss them with the vinegar and season to taste with salt.

Cut out and discard the ribs from the lettuce leaves, halving each leaf.

In a shallow baking pan or cake pan, soak 2 rice paper rounds in hot water until very pliable—45 seconds to 1 minute.

Carefully spread 1 soaked round on a paper towel, leaving the remaining round in the water, and blot with another paper towel. Arrange 1 piece of lettuce leaf on the bottom half of the round, leaving a 1-inch border along the edge. Top the lettuce with about one-fourth of the crushed peanuts and one-fourth of the noodles, arranging them in a line across the lettuce. Top the noodles with one-fourth each of the green onion, carrot, cabbage, and herbs. Roll the bottom of the rice paper up tightly over the filling once, fold the sides in, and then continue rolling up the filling tightly in the rice paper.

Spread the remaining soaked rice paper round on a paper towel and blot. Wrap the rice paper around the rolled spring roll in the same manner. (Double wrapping covers any tears and makes the roll more stable and easier to eat.) Wrap up the spring roll in a rinsed and squeezed paper towel and put it in a resealable plastic bag. Make three more rolls with the remaining

RECIPE: HERB SALAD SPRING ROLLS

ingredients. Rolls may be made 1 day ahead and refrigerated, wrapped in wet paper towels and sealed in a plastic bag.

Before serving, bring the rolls to room temperature. Discard the paper towels. Halve the rolls diagonally and serve with peanut sauce.

Spicy Peanut Sauce

This sauce is the must-have accompaniment for the Herb Salad Spring Rolls but can also be used as a dipping sauce for chicken satay or a topping for cold noodles!

3 garlic cloves, minced
¼ teaspoon red pepper flakes
1 tablespoon vegetable oil
1 tablespoon tomato paste
3 tablespoons creamy peanut butter
3 tablespoons hoisin sauce
½ teaspoon sugar
¾ cup water

Makes 1 cup

In a small saucepan, cook the garlic and red pepper flakes in oil over moderate heat, stirring, until the garlic is golden, 2 to 3 minutes.

Add the remaining ingredients and bring to a boil, whisking. Simmer the sauce, whisking constantly, until thickened, about 1 minute. Sauce may be made 3 days ahead and refrigerated, covered.

Serve sauce warm or at room temperature.

Spicy Tuna Tartare on Wonton Crisps

This recipe is always a crowd pleaser and definitely has a wow factor. Bake your wonton crisps, dice your tuna, and make your sauce all ahead of time. Combine them when you're ready to serve.

1 teaspoon vegetable oil
Wonton squares, cut in half diagonally
10 ounces sushi grade tuna, diced into small pieces*
3 tablespoons chopped green onions
3 tablespoons toasted pine nuts
1 tablespoon plus 1 teaspoon soy sauce
1 tablespoon sesame oil
1½ teaspoons minced jalapeño (no seeds)
1 teaspoon grated, peeled fresh ginger

Makes 48 pieces

Preheat the oven to 350°F.

Brush a baking sheet with the oil.

Arrange the wonton wrappers on the sheet and bake until golden, 8 to 10 minutes. Watch closely—they burn very easily.

Combine the tuna, green onion, pine nuts, soy sauce, sesame oil, jalapeño, and ginger. Mix well.

Top each wonton crisp with about 1 tablespoon of the tuna tartare and serve immediately.

*Sushi grade tuna will always be frozen. Cutting the tuna into a small dice is easier to do when it's still frozen. Let it defrost before mixing it with the remaining ingredients.

Caramelized Onion Dip

I have a serious potato chip addiction—I got it from my mom. This dip is so delicious, and it's the perfect accompaniment to a big bag of salty, crunchy chips. I suppose if you had to, you could use this dip with fresh vegetables . . . if you had to.

4 tablespoons unsalted butter
¼ cup vegetable oil
2 large yellow onions, halved and sliced thinly
⅛ teaspoon cayenne pepper
1 teaspoon kosher salt
½ teaspoon pepper
4 ounces cream cheese, at room temperature
½ cup sour cream
½ cup good mayonnaise

Makes 1½ cups

Heat the butter and oil in a large sauté pan on medium-high heat. Add the onions, cayenne, salt, and pepper and sauté for 8 to 10 minutes, until the onions start to develop a nice color. Reduce the heat to medium-low and cook, stirring occasionally, for 20 more minutes, or until the onions are browned and caramelized. Allow them to cool.

In the bowl of an electric mixer fitted with a paddle attachment, beat the cream cheese, sour cream, and mayonnaise until smooth. Add the onions and mix well. Season with salt and pepper.

Serve at room temperature with your favorite potato chips!

Heirloom Tomato and Nectarine Salad with Whipped Feta

There is nothing better than cooking seasonally and taking advantage of produce at the height of its freshness. This salad is made incredible by using end-of-summer, perfectly ripe tomatoes and nectarines.

¾ cup crumbled feta cheese (about ⅓ pound)
¼ cup whole milk
2 teaspoons extra-virgin olive oil plus more for drizzling
2 nectarines, quartered and sliced into wedges
1 pound heirloom tomatoes, sliced ½ inch thick and halved
¼ cup Marcona almonds
¼ cup fresh mint, coarsely chopped
¼ cup flat-leaf parsley
Flaky sea salt

Makes 6–8 servings

In the bowl of a small food processor, combine the feta, milk, and olive oil and process until smooth. Press the cheese through a fine-mesh strainer set over a small bowl to remove any cheese crumbles. The mixture should be very smooth.

Add the whipped feta to a large serving plate and top with the nectarine and tomato slices. Sprinkle the almonds on top and drizzle the fruit lightly with olive oil.

Finish by garnishing with the chopped mint and parsley and a sprinkling of flaky sea salt to serve.

Grilled Squash Ribbons and Prosciutto with Mint Dressing

I love when a recipe yields huge results with only minimal effort and ingredients; this summer appetizer does exactly that. Don't step away from the grill once you place these skewers on—they will be ready before you know it!

2 medium zucchini
2 medium yellow squash
1 teaspoon finely grated lime zest
¼ cup fresh lime juice
¼ cup chopped mint
2 garlic cloves, very finely chopped
¼ cup extra-virgin olive oil plus more for brushing
6 ounces thinly sliced prosciutto

Makes 4 servings

Light a grill or preheat a grill pan.

Very thinly slice the zucchini and yellow squash lengthwise on a mandoline.

In a small bowl, combine the lime zest and juice with the mint, garlic, and olive oil. Season with salt and pepper.

Alternately thread the zucchini, yellow squash, and prosciutto onto four pairs of 12-inch bamboo skewers. Lightly brush the vegetables and prosciutto with olive oil and season generously with salt and pepper.

Grill the skewers over high heat until the zucchini and yellow squash are lightly charred, about 1½ minutes per side. Serve with the mint dressing on the side.

PART VI

IT'S COMPLICATED

Vive la France!

What's your favorite food to cook?

I love this question.

Actually, I hate this question.

Which is to say, I have a love-hate relationship with this question.

I wish I could just answer with "Gin and tonics" and be done with it, but I know that's not the kind of response people are looking for. Okay, yes, it's charming, it's affirming, it's a compliment to be asked such a question. I'm honored to be asked.

But it's so *limiting*. When you cook for a living—when people pay you to prepare food for them—your favorite foods don't really matter much. Professional cooks rarely cook for themselves, more often opting for pizza or Chinese takeout or whatever happens to be left in the fridge. Perhaps the better question, though still difficult to answer, is: What's your favorite food to eat?

I've been fortunate to have many and varied dining experiences. I've eaten sitting on a dirt floor in a remote village in Chiang Mai, with a topless woman breastfeeding next to me. I've enjoyed freshly caught pirarucu in the rainforests of Ecuador, as well as some of the best pizza I've ever tasted at one o'clock in the morning on the streets of Florence.

Hold my feet to a fire and force me to answer, and I'll say: I love French food.

I've never experienced anything more consistently impressive, more deeply moving, more truly inspiring, than French food.

And while you can certainly have amazing mussels in Brittany, outstanding omelets in Normandy, and perfect pissaladière in Marseille, Paris has always been my place.

Since when?

Long ago.

Why?

I'll take you there.

My love affair with Paris is now in its fourth decade. I was single when I first went, in my late twenties. I had just bought my first house—well, half a house, a three-family walk-up above my grandparents' beloved East Boston store, purchased when they decided to retire and move to the suburbs.

Buying that half a house and then going to Paris meant I had a "big ass." At least according to my mother.

In my family, this phrase, *big ass*, had nothing to do with the actual physical size of someone's anatomical backside. *Big ass* referred to the sin of excess, of living beyond your means. Not an actual sin. Not a Catholic sin. Not venial, not cardinal. It was just . . . well, more like this: Freddy buys a fancy new car? "Look at that! Ain't Freddy got a big ass!"

So when I bought my first-ever house and then booked a trip to Europe *in the same year*, my mother's response was inevitable: "Well, excuse me; look at my son and his big ass!" But I went. Big ass and all.

Not actually to Paris. At least not at first. The original plan, the original sin, was a vacation in London. London was safe. English speaking. I happened to have a little money in my pocket and I was single, and I figured I'd visit London.

But Mirna did not approve. First my mother, now Mirna. Why, I don't know, but during this time, the women in my life didn't seem to approve of my plans.

I was still working at Suffolk University—just a production assistant in the theater department, with students swirling all around me. One student was Mirna from Paris, of Iranian descent, with a beautiful Persian look and an exquisite French accent.

She was the classic Parisian snob. *"Vous êtes qui? Ah, je ne te connais pas."* (Classic Parisian snub.)

So when she learned that I was planning a vacation in London, she snorted. "Why would you go to London?" No, maybe more of a snarl: "Why wouldn't you go to Paris?"

Mirna didn't stop there. She taunted me. "If you were going to Paris," she announced, "I would give you the keys to my apartment."

I did a double take.

Her father had been a political type; her mother owned an antique shop. As it turns out, her parents kept an apartment for Mirna above the shop.

It was sitting there, empty, waiting for me.

Mirna kept taunting me.

I was very green, but... London to Paris, a three-hour train ride. I figured I could do that.

Mirna gave me the address of her mother's antique shop. Her mother, she said, would give me the key. Also, one word of advice: Her mother loved Dentyne chewing gum, and she couldn't get it in France. Take her a gift.

I went to Costco. I bought an enormous box of Dentyne. I got on a plane and flew to London. I got on a train and went to Paris.

I got in a taxi—faithfully carrying my supersized box of chewing gum—and, employing absolutely terrible French, asked the driver to stop at a flower shop. Which is how I ended up at an antique shop owned by a total stranger, handing her a box of gum and a bouquet of flowers, kissing her lightly on each cheek and then taking a key from her, and ascending the stairs to Mirna's apartment.

It was very dark, very bohemian. It was clear that Mirna's mother was using this space for a number of antiques that hadn't sold. One piece, a very disturbing painting, midcentury Persian, depicted a gang of women with daggers repeatedly stabbing a man. It hung over the bed.

I'm going to sleep here?

The fridge was empty, but the freezer featured the biggest bag of Iranian pistachios I've ever seen. I could eat ice-cold pistachios to my heart's content.

Which I did. I was in heaven—till I went to an Irish pub and got punched in the face.

It was the James Joyce Pub. Not exactly a Parisian name. But what did I know?

In the course of an otherwise innocuous tourist-type evening, I accidentally bumped a gentleman's arm, and his drink sloshed about.

My own command of the French language was somewhere between terrible and nonexistent, but I'm quite sure the victim was ranting in French, and for quite some time.

I apologized profusely, as profusely as one can apologize in terrible, nonexistent French, and offered to buy him another beer, but to no avail. Eventually I heard English—very accented English, but recognizable: "Fucking American."

In that moment, I guess I hit the wall, the limit of my humanitarian instincts, and I said—in perfect English—"Fuck you."

And he punched me in the face.

I would like to tell you that a wild European barroom brawl ensued, I'd love to tell you that I landed a punch in return, but no. Suddenly, the bartender was calling the cops, sirens were sounding in the street. Holding my face, I dodged into the street and headed back to my dark, totally safe little borrowed apartment with pistachios, where women were stabbing some guy.

The next day, paranoid about the possibility of dealing with the French authorities, I bid Mirna's mom au revoir, got on the train heading back to London, and booked myself a room in an even safer English-speaking Marriott.

Yet the Paris bug had bitten.

It was a magical place (forgive me for the cliché, but it was).

Then, regret. I got home to the US and told myself I'd been a wimp, I shouldn't have fled. I should have done it, à la Sinatra, *my way*.

So the next year, I went back.

Since then and every year after, nothing but love.

Yes, I was looking at life through a much different lens back then, in the beginning, as a young single guy. But however it happened, I fell in love with Paris—and I continued going back. My life changed, I got older, I met Bob, we went to Paris together, we became parents, we kept going back to Paris. Different lenses, different ages, different perspectives—yet Paris was somehow still, always, wonderful. Paris kept offering me something new. Paris kept meeting me wherever I was in life, and inspiring new, bold strokes.

As well as old, familiar strokes. Mirna and I still talk and visit with each other—she's married with three children, living in Switzerland. And to this day, I can't go to Paris without visiting Mirna's mother and eating Persian food at her magnificent dining room table.

So it was probably inevitable that Christopher's Table would launch cooking tours of Paris. This was another in a long line of beyond-the-storefront experiments. *If muffins can't pay the bills, what can—and still be fun, still be about food, still be true to me? If someone in Ipswich, Massachusetts, doesn't want my prepared foods, do I just write them off? No. This is about people. What do they want? Are they not buying prepared foods because they love to cook? Would they like a cooking class? A wine dinner? Do they want to come to a drag show?*

My mind was always churning through the possibilities, creative ways to connect with people, and generate buzz, and, of course, pay the bills.

Until I arrived at the possibility of Paris. A culinary tour. *Would people actually pay me to visit Paris?* Nonsense.

Let's try it.

People entrusting enormous amounts of money to me to lead an international expedition—this was a crazy idea.

So I went into it with a fatalistic perspective: *If no one signs up, so be it.*

Mirna, who had since graduated from Suffolk University and moved back to Paris, was working in the hospitality industry and connected me with a company specializing in such tours. The company assigned me a liaison who quizzed me about my objectives, then mapped out options. I would fly over several months in advance, visit a number of hotels, meet restaurant chefs, and test-drive a few cooking classes. With Mirna as my faithful sidekick, I would assess the pricing, select restaurants and hotels, and determine the schedule. (Mirna was invaluable. She was my personal French negotiator: "Dinner for fifteen will cost how much? That's screwy. We'll do it for half that.")

And then, with the plan set, I began talking.

I talked to customers. And prospective customers. I talked to my Ipswich cooking classes. I chatted it up on social media.

"Wanna do a private cooking class with me in Paris?" Crazy idea. I knew it wouldn't work.

When the first person signed up, I was stunned. My initial response was *Jeez, this is real.* Then, almost immediately, I calculated the downside. *If no one else signs up, I'll have to refund this money and confess to my failure.*

I knew my "magic number." I knew how many people I would need to break even. How many people I needed to make the trip viable. Maybe, if I squeaked by, I could learn from my dismal mistakes and come home and regroup and do better next time.

Chris, who do you think you are, making such a far-fetched offer? Big ass! Then came the others.

Two people, five people, ten people! I was still giddy about ten people signing up when numbers eleven and twelve deposited. *Who are these people?*

Holy cow. Look at all these people signing up! Yet I couldn't even enjoy my success. I started fretting about the future.

What if these people all got to France and didn't like the tour I had planned? The restaurants I had picked? What if they didn't get along? *I'm responsible for their enjoyment! They could hate each other!*

So I staged a required cocktail party. A meet-and-greet orientation event where I gathered all the tour guests at Christopher's Table some weeks before departure.

Somehow, it worked. I was simultaneously scared shitless and utterly delighted. The dream kept coming together.

Our group, on this first venture, was a good mix, thank heaven. Couples and solo women, and a pair of women traveling together who planned to springboard off the Christopher's Table tour and venture to Italy. It all worked.

The plan, on paper, was simple. Get yourself to the lobby of our hotel in Paris (I don't do travel agent stuff, sorry), then from that moment on—two o'clock on a certain afternoon—you have no other responsibilities, no other costs, unless you decide to buy souvenirs. Carry cash in your pocket, if you wish. Otherwise, you don't need a wallet until the end of our tour. And then, at the end, a farewell reception in the lobby of the same hotel where we started.

Five days. Enjoy it.

I wasn't satisfied with the basics. Hooking up with the tour company that Mirna recommended, I could have settled for a bus. But I wanted our Christopher's Table guests to have a more rarefied experience. Our group was too small for a tacky tour bus and too large for most other vehicles, so we settled on a Mercedes minivan. This was the kind of detail I thrived on.

"This is not a tourism tour!" I announced to our group. "This is not seeing the Eiffel Tower, wandering the Louvre, taking selfies at Notre-Dame. There will be calendar segments set aside for that stuff on your own. But *this tour*? It's purely culinary. This is what you signed up for. Cooking. Cookerism. Cookoscopy. Don't make me keep inventing words."

Some days, we settled for breakfast at the hotel. But that was not typical. Every day, we were fully mapped out for lunch and dinner. And it wasn't just local neighborhood Paris stuff. We might launch into a two-hour drive to the Champagne region for a tour of the Veuve Clicquot champagne house, then lunch in a small village in Reims, then a cheese place. And what next? Everything was planned, but felt spontaneous!

One morning, we arranged in advance to wake up at 4:00 a.m. for a jaunt to the wholesale food markets that serve metro Paris restaurants. Walk into this extravagant, otherworldly space, and you'll find yourself in a swirl of fish caught just an hour ago, fresh flowers, absolutely gorgeous produce—anything a chef might need.

I was astounded. Almost paralyzed with joy and astonishment. I couldn't help but flash back to the chaotic food markets I'd shopped in Boston. By comparison, they were disgusting. Dirty. Rude and loud, with forklifts and wilting lettuce on the floor. I'd been visiting such places in Massachusetts since I was a child, with my grandfather. But here, in France, was a different approach. Thrilling. Artistic, almost. Breathtaking displays. Multicolored radishes, thoughtfully and purposefully arranged. And clean! You could eat off the floor.

In my stupor, in a moment away from my group, I met a local woman.

"I've spent a lot of time in the US in places like this," I said to her, "and they don't look anything like this."

She gave me a stern look for a moment or two, then offered her assessment: "It's because in America, you do not respect food."

And in that moment, I knew she was right. But I came to respect French food. And the French food industry. Hugely. Because the food—the taste and the production of it—was unerringly spectacular.

It helped that Mirna had set me up with a superb tour company. So our visits to French restaurants were completely planned by our expert handlers and painstakingly vetted by *moi*. This was not a

Beautiful displays at Rungis Market, the world's second-largest wholesale produce market, located just outside of Paris—also the principal wholesale market for Paris itself

matter of walking into a restaurant and asking, "Do you have a table for thirteen?" Everything was beautifully arranged.

But I did learn some lessons from that first tour:

1. Americans need coffee first thing in the morning. When you make them wake up at 4:00 a.m. to visit a market, you probably should arrange for them to have coffee before they get into the van—or at least once they've staggered into the van.
2. Perhaps I was overzealous in my development of the itinerary. I only came to this conclusion because people were totally, genuinely exhausted. I was high-anxiety about the fact that these people had paid thousands of dollars each, plus airfare; I didn't want them to have buyer's remorse.
3. Overseas tours are really complicated.

Fauchon, a famous catering company based in Paris, offers a pink equivalent of the Tiffany Blue Box. If you find a beautiful blue Tiffany box or a fabulous pink Fauchon box in your hotel room, you know you've been well cared for. Fauchon was well known for their delectable prepared food! So I arranged to have big pink boxes filled with duck terrine, salmon mousse, and macarons waiting in each of our guests' hotel rooms upon their arrival. They didn't even have to go out to get something to eat if they were hungry. Bon appétit, welcome to Paris—even before the tour begins!

Everyone arrived at different times. Mercifully accounting for travel fatigue and the onset of jet lag, I wanted to give people time to decompress, relax, maybe even walk around the neighborhood if they wanted.

Pre-dinner, we gathered as a group for the first time in the lobby. A champagne toast officially kicked off our adventure, and then we went to our first restaurant dinner. Mirna and I had selected the entire menu in advance. As we were all seated, servers brought a grand supply of French bread to the table. Mirna reached for a piece and immediately returned it to its basket. She called to the server.

"Ce n'est pas frais!" This bread is not fresh!

I freaked out a bit. "What are you doing?"

"Non," she growled. "They think you're just a bunch of Americans, so they can give you stale bread."

All the baskets disappeared. New baskets, with *frais* bread, soon appeared. Mirna is a force to be reckoned with.

Touring a "meat hall," I was enchanted. Can raw meat be gorgeous? I think so. Huge chunks of dead cows were hanging on hooks, and I loved them, each and every one. The color, the texture, the sheer raw meatiness of it all.

It clearly wasn't the United States; there was no FDA here. Yes, I was wearing a hairnet and a white lab coat, but forget about gloves. At a massive counter, a worker proudly offered a slab of meat and urged me to note the marbling, feel the texture! No, John Q. Public doesn't typically get excited about wholesale food markets. To me, it was a highlight—maybe *the* highlight—of that first Paris culinary tour.

Participants of our culinary tour about to enter Rungis Market at its daily opening at 4:15 a.m.

Meanwhile, my traveling companions were thrilled to visit the famous 200-year-old E. Dehillerin cookware store on rue Coquilliere, equidistant from the nearby Louvre and Marais neighborhood. Copper saucepans, mandolines, molds, terrines! Whisks ranging in size from *très très petit* to the size of a young child!

I loved seeing my guests so happy. But for me? No. *It was the meat.*

So we survived the debut tour. Yes, there were stress points, or problems here and there, embarrassing moments. But the participants were sensitive. They could see what I was going through. From time to time, someone would quietly rub my back and say, "It's okay."

And yes, it was okay. It was more than okay. It was beautiful.

Now, to the business. The accounting. The money.

Frankly, the margin was small. But if I could get enough people signed up for a culinary tour of Paris, it would be worth it to put a sign on the door at Christopher's Table for a week—*Closed for a Paris culinary tour*—and go to Paris. *Go to Paris!* Five days of eating and drinking in *Paris*. To be honest, I loved being able to say, if only to myself, *I'm gonna be working for the next five days in Paris!* My Bob is still rolling his eyes!

Ultimately, however, arranging a tour—even with Mirna, even with expert help in Paris—required innumerable hours of administrative work. This wasn't the kind of work that you could hand off to a sous-chef. This involved phone time, accounting for US-to-Europe time zones, converting costs from euros to dollars, and on and on. And I was, bottom line, a one-man operation. A tour to Paris could be profitable moneywise but draining timewise.

And all the fun at home, the energy on Depot Square, the buzz at Christopher's Table, the jazz back in Ipswich, Massachusetts . . . it called me home.

VIVE LA FRANCE!

French 75 Cocktail

Named after a 75 mm Howitzer field gun used by the French and the Americans in World War I. The gun was known for its accuracy and speed, and the French 75 is said to have a kick that feels like being hit by just such a weapon. An early form was created in 1915 at the New York Bar in Paris—later Harry's New York Bar.

1½ ounces gin, such as Hendrick's
¾ ounce fresh lemon juice
¾ ounce simple syrup
2 ounces champagne
Long spiral lemon twist (garnish)

Makes 1 serving

Combine the gin, lemon juice, and simple syrup in a cocktail shaker. Fill the shaker with ice, cover, and shake vigorously until the outside of the shaker is very cold, about 20 seconds.

Strain the cocktail through a Hawthorne strainer or a slotted spoon into a large flute. Top with champagne; garnish with a lemon twist.

Gougères—French Cheese Puffs

When the very first group arrived in Paris for our Christopher's Table culinary tour, we had a kick-off celebration in the lobby of the Lutetia hotel. We toasted our adventure with champagne and these baked savory choux pastries mixed with Gruyère cheese.

- 1 cup plus 1 tablespoon whole milk, divided
- 8 tablespoons unsalted butter
- ½ teaspoon kosher salt
- 1 cup all-purpose flour
- 5 large eggs plus 1 yolk, at room temperature, divided
- 3 ounces grated Parmigiano-Reggiano cheese, divided
- 3 ounces grated Gruyère cheese
- 1 tablespoon fresh thyme leaves, finely chopped

Makes 24-30 pieces

Preheat the oven to 400°F and arrange the racks in the upper and lower third.

Line two rimmed baking sheets with parchment paper or silicone baking mats and set aside.

Combine 1 cup of the milk with the butter and salt in a medium saucepan and bring it to a simmer over medium-high heat. Reduce the heat to medium-low, dump in the flour, and stir vigorously until the flour is incorporated. Cook, stirring constantly, until the dough comes together in a ball and feels dry to the touch, about 2 minutes.

Transfer the dough to a food processor fitted with a blade or a stand mixer fitted with a paddle attachment. Pulse or beat in the five eggs, one by one, letting each egg completely incorporate before adding the next. Reserve 3 tablespoons of the Parmigiano-Reggiano cheese, then add the remaining Parmigiano-Reggiano, Gruyère, and thyme; pulse or mix on low until thoroughly incorporated.

Drop tablespoon-size portions of dough on the prepared baking sheets (I use a very small ice cream scoop), spacing them at least ½ inch apart. Whisk the remaining egg yolk with the remaining 1 tablespoon milk and brush it on top of the cheese puffs, then evenly sprinkle the reserved Parmigiano-Reggiano over the top.

Bake, rotating the baking sheets halfway through, until puffed and golden brown, 20 to 25 minutes. Serve hot, warm, or at room temperature.

Quiche au Fromage

Although quiche is known as a dish of classic French cuisine, historical records indicate that quiche actually originated in Germany in the middle ages in the medieval kingdom of Lothringen, which the French later occupied and renamed Lorraine. The word *quiche* is from the German *Kuchen*, meaning "cake." While some people love to split hairs about its origin, I will settle for its being delicious!

- 1 basic pastry crust recipe
- 6 large eggs
- ⅔ cup heavy cream or crème fraîche
- 1 cup milk (preferably whole)
- 1 teaspoon salt
- 1 teaspoon pepper
- 8 ounces Gruyère, Emmenthal, or other Swiss-type cheese
- ¼ teaspoon freshly ground nutmeg (optional)

Makes 6–8 servings

Roll out the pastry and fit into a 10½-inch glass or metal pie plate (not one with a removable bottom). Crimp the edges, poke the bottom with a fork or the tip of a sharp knife, and place the pastry in the freezer for 30 minutes.

Preheat the oven to 425°F. Line the pastry with aluminum foil, fill with pastry weights, and bake in the bottom third of the oven until golden at the edges, about 15 minutes.

Remove from the oven and remove the foil and pastry weights.

Return the pastry to the oven to bake until the bottom is golden, an additional 5 minutes. Remove from the oven.

In a medium-sized bowl, whisk together the eggs, cream, and milk until thoroughly blended. Add the salt, pepper, and cheese and stir until blended.

Spread the mixture in the prebaked pastry. Sprinkle with nutmeg (if you've used a Swiss-type cheese) and bake in the center of the oven until the filling is golden and puffed and completely baked through, about 30 minutes.

To test for doneness, shake the quiche—if it's solid without a pool of uncooked filling in the center, it is done. You may also stick a sharp knife blade into the center of the filling, and if it comes out clean, the quiche is baked through.

Remove the quiche from the oven and serve immediately.

Moules Frites

Moules frites literally translates to "mussels and french fries," which is one of my favorite combinations. There is nothing better than sitting in an outdoor café in Paris with a glass of wine, a big bowl of fresh mussels, and crispy fries.

14 ounces store-bought frozen french fries
1 cup mayonnaise
2 teaspoons Dijon mustard
4 tablespoons unsalted butter
1 large shallot, finely chopped
4 garlic cloves, minced
2 teaspoons kosher salt
2 cups dry white wine
3 pounds mussels
2 tablespoons parsley, roughly chopped
Lemon wedges, for serving

Makes 4 servings

Cook the french fries according to the package instructions.

While the fries cook, combine the mayonnaise and Dijon mustard in a medium bowl and whisk until smooth.

Melt the butter in a large Dutch oven over medium heat. Add the shallot, garlic, and salt and cook until softened and translucent, about 3 minutes.

Add the wine and bring to a simmer. Add the mussels and stir to coat them in the aromatics.

Cover the pot and cook until the mussels just begin to open, about 5 minutes.

Taste the cooking liquid and add salt as needed. Top the mussels with parsley and serve with lemon wedges alongside french fries and Dijon-mayonnaise dipping sauce.

Brussels Sprouts Lardons

Our culinary tours through Paris included some absolutely amazing restaurants. One that stands out was Le Procope. This brasserie is steeped in history, having been in the sixth arrondissement since 1686. While it's widely known for being where the greatest writers and intellectuals gathered, I remember it for the small copper terrine of sweet, nutty brussels sprouts and smoky lardons we had as a side dish for lunch.

2 tablespoons good olive oil
6 ounces Italian pancetta diced small (about ¼ inch)
2 pounds brussels sprouts, trimmed and cut in half
1 teaspoon kosher salt
1 tablespoon brown sugar
¾ teaspoon pepper
1¾ cups chicken stock

Makes 4-6 servings

Heat the olive oil in a large sauté pan, then add the pancetta. Cook over medium heat, stirring often, until the fat is rendered and the pancetta is golden brown and crisp, 5 to 10 minutes. Remove the pancetta from the pan and set aside.

Add the brussels sprouts, salt, brown sugar, and pepper to the fat in the pan and sauté over medium heat for about 5 minutes, or until lightly browned.

Add the chicken stock. Lower the heat and cook uncovered, stirring occasionally, until the sprouts are tender when pierced with a knife, about 15 minutes. If the skillet becomes too dry, add a little chicken stock or water.

Return the pancetta to the pan and cook until heated through.

Season with salt and pepper and serve.

French Strawberry Tart

In my mind, walking into a French bakery is equivalent to walking into an art museum—I could stay and look at all the beautiful things for hours. I fell in love with this custard-filled fruit tart on our very first culinary tour, and we've been together ever since.

Pastry cream:
- 2 cups whole milk
- 1 vanilla bean, split lengthwise, or 1 teaspoon vanilla extract
- 5 large egg yolks
- 6 to 8 tablespoons sugar
- 3 tablespoons all-purpose flour
- 3 tablespoons cornstarch

Tart:
- 1¼ cups pastry cream
- 1 medium baked sweet pastry shell (pâte sucrée)
- 1 pound strawberries, whole or sliced
- ¼ cup strawberry jam
- 1 tablespoon lemon juice or water

Makes 6–8 servings

In a medium-sized saucepan, heat the milk and the vanilla bean (if using) over medium heat almost to boiling.

While the milk is heating, mix the egg yolks and sugar in a large bowl. Whisk in the flour and cornstarch until the mixture is smooth.

Remove the vanilla bean from the milk. Gradually whisk the hot milk into the egg mixture. Do this very slowly, as you don't want the yolks to cook from the heat of the milk.

Strain the mixture back into the saucepan. Cook over medium heat, constantly stirring or whisking, until the mixture thickens and reaches a boil. Continue cooking for 30 seconds longer, stirring hard and continuously to keep the pastry cream smooth.

Remove from the heat. Stir in the vanilla flavoring now if you did not use a vanilla bean.

Place a layer of plastic wrap directly on the surface of the pastry cream to avoid a skin forming, and leave it to cool to room temperature. The pastry cream can be used when cool, or covered and refrigerated up to several days until needed. Stir the chilled pastry cream before using.

To put together the tart, spread the pastry cream across the bottom of the baked sweet pastry shell. Arrange the strawberries in a pattern over the cream.

Heat the strawberry jam and lemon juice until boiling. Use a pastry brush to apply the strawberry glaze to the strawberries.

Refrigerate the tart for several hours before serving.

Chocolate Pots de Crème

The French love their dairy products: yogurts of all kinds and what they call the *crèmes desserts*. French supermarkets devote entire refrigerated aisles to yogurts, fromages blancs, flans, mousses, and all kinds of custards and heavenly pots de crème. These classic French Chocolate Pots de Crème are made of the simplest ingredients and baked in a water bath to produce a creamy custard, with only the top of the pots "baking" in a dry heat to create a thicker, skin-like surface.

2 cups whipping cream
½ cup whole milk
5 ounces bittersweet or semisweet chocolate, chopped
6 large egg yolks
⅓ cup sugar

Makes 6 servings

Preheat the oven to 325°F.

Bring the cream and milk just to a simmer in a heavy medium-sized saucepan over medium heat. Remove from the heat. Add the chocolate and whisk until melted and smooth.

Whisk the yolks and sugar in a large bowl to blend. Gradually whisk in the hot chocolate mixture. Strain the mixture into another bowl. Cool for 10 minutes, skimming any foam from the surface.

Divide the custard mixture among 6 (¾-cup) custard cups or soufflé dishes. Cover each with foil.

Place the cups in a large baking pan. Add enough hot water to the pan to come halfway up the sides of the cups. Bake until the custards are set but the centers still move slightly when gently shaken, about 55 minutes. Remove the cups from the water. Remove the foil.

Refrigerate the custards until cold, about 3 hours. The pots de crème can be made 2 days ahead. Cover and keep refrigerated.

VIVE LA FRANCE!

CORRAL THE QUEENS

PART VII

Buy Someone a Drink

January and February in Massachusetts are dark and cold. It's post-holidays, people tend to hibernate, they're not out spending money—all of which makes it a dark time for most businesses, let alone a small retail food shop.

To keep cash flowing—to appeal to a broader demographic, to reach people who didn't care a bit about my prepared foods—I experimented with imagining and inventing events. What would bring people out to a food shop? What would be fun? I was still throwing things at the wall to see what would stick. How about a Crazy Sexy Chocolate Party? What does that even entail? I didn't know because I was making it up as I went. How about a Western-themed party called Giddy Up, featuring beautiful shirtless men wearing chaps and leather vests? How about a beach party, with cabana boys in swim trunks passing hors d'oeuvres? How about a burlesque show? Whatever worked, I did again the next winter. Whatever didn't work went the way Dylan Thomas advised against: gentle into that good night.

Ipswich surprised me. In many ways it's a provincial place, with a classic prudish, small-town mentality. But people rolled the dice and came out to Christopher's Table to throw dollar bills at a drag queen or investigate an evening of crazy sexy chocolate.

My space was small, so there was a serious occupancy limit. But if an event sold out, I made good money. And when I found that drag shows routinely (and almost immediately) sold out—the kind of show you'd normally have to go into Boston for—I began bringing up more and more drag stars from the city. Locals soon discovered that they had to snap up tickets quickly, as soon as an event was announced, because they'd be gone in hours—or minutes.

I learned the hard way that queens are notoriously late—unreliable, unpredictable—and yes, that's a stereotype, and yes, I'm willing to go on the record with it. I'd find myself, at five minutes to showtime, asking, "Where's Dusty Bureau?" So I began ordering a limo service to pick up my performers in Boston and deliver them to Christopher's Table's doorstep. It was an added expense, but it was worth it, because it was the only way to know that I was going to get the entire cast of queens at the appointed time.

Which was usually about 4:00 p.m., broad daylight. I put a sign on the door—*Closed for our sold-out drag show*. People drinking early at the May Flower bar next door thought it was the greatest show on earth: they could stand on the sidewalk, smoking cigarettes, and watch drag queens falling out of a limousine with suitcases and wigs and straggling into my shop.

I had to black out the shop windows too, because people congregated on the sidewalk trying to steal a glimpse of those sequined, bra-stuffing beauties from Boston.

One evening, I tested the prudish local mentality more directly than I really cared to. I brought in a number of performers from Boston, and found one of them—stage name Miranda Wrights, by light of day, a very attractive man named Bobby—to be exceptionally wild, flirty, and fun. And even before the show began, a drinker. Also during the show. Oh well, it didn't really matter, did it? These queens had no memorized lines to deliver—they were lip-synching.

Midshow, Miranda Wrights came to the end of a number, headed back into the kitchen-turned-dressing room (shhh, don't tell the local board of health), leaned over to me, and said, "We're going out for a drink after this, aren't we?"

I was surprised, but not opposed. "Sure, yeah." I shrugged. "We can."

Fast-forward to the end of the show. Applause, bows, boa feathers, the crowd begins dispersing.

"So where are we gonna go?" Miranda asked, still in drag.

"I don't know," I replied. "There's nothing fancy in Ipswich. Maybe the May Flower? It's a Chinese restaurant next door. Kind of a dive, but we can get a drink at the bar."

"Perfect!" Miranda announced. "Let's go!"

My heart stopped. I was expecting to have a drink with Bobby. I wasn't counting on making an appearance with Miranda Wrights herself, fully decked out in drag—makeup, wig, dress. It was only a few steps from the front door of Christopher's Table to the front door of the May Flower, but in those few seconds I had some serious calculating to do. I think it's fair to describe the typical May Flower bar crowd as, shall we say, perhaps on the somewhat socially conservative side, and perhaps somewhat outspoken, and perhaps somewhat argumentative. So I could easily imagine a somewhat negative reaction to our entrance and to my friend.

Before we arrived at the May Flower door, I paused.

"I have a question," I said to my date. "Can you fight in those heels?"

Miranda gave me a leering snort. "Hell yeah, I can fight."

I took a deep breath. "Okay! Let's go!"

Left: *Debauchery and shenanigans with the ladies; clockwise left to right: Crystal Crawford, Kris Knievel, and Rainbow Fright;* Right: *Kris Knievel takes center stage*

The next few moments were like a scene from a movie. The bar starts at the front door and stretches away from you, the full length of the room. As we walked in, every head at the bar, from near to far, swiveled in our direction. And every face momentarily dropped in silent astonishment. I swallowed hard as Miranda confidently made her way to the bar.

But then came the Ipswich surprise. Everybody loved Miranda Wrights. The women at the bar, most of all, gushed. "I love your hair!" "I love that dress!" "Where did you get those?" "Fabulous!" The men at the bar behaved as gentlemen.

Miranda Wrights's drag-queen persona was not an issue.

And I didn't get beat up.

Win-win.

And then I painted the walls red. I hung chandeliers. I turned Christopher's Table into a wine bar.

It wasn't really that sudden. Special events had turned Christopher's Table into something of a venue, a local destination. It seemed I could gather people—my age-old longing—and if I could snag a beer and wine license, I could put in a bar and gather even *more* people.

Getting the license wasn't a foregone conclusion. There are only so many licenses available, under state regulations, and you have to wait for an opening. Then you have to plead your case before the elected leaders, and they have to approve you. Or not.

But leaders in Ipswich—I don't necessarily mean politicians and bureaucrats, I mean longtime residents, gatekeepers, who quietly make things happen behind the scenes—pulled for me. The attitude seemed to be, *Christopher's a good guy, he hasn't failed yet. Yeah, drag queens in Ipswich is a little crazy—but it's Christopher. Who knows? He'll probably make this work.*

So the Town of Ipswich graciously granted me a license, for which I was truly grateful; and I reconfigured my space, installed a bar and a small couch and a few little tables, and voilà! We had a wine bar coexisting with a prepared-foods shop.

There were awkward moments. A customer might arrive looking for our wonderful salmon, only to find a bar full of people drinking wine. Eventually I tried partitioning: baked goods during the day, and then at 4:30, the baked-goods case shut down, the lights dimmed, the music was piped in, and I started serving wine.

Of course, before long, it was clear that a case of muffins and steak tips doesn't hold a candle to the profit margin on wine and beer. I was getting up early every morning, the happy little muffin maker of yore, and staying up late at the bar every night, and gradually ruining myself and ignoring my family.

Ultimately, I said goodbye to my prepared foods, trading in my steak tips for a nice bottle of pinot noir and making way for a reimagined Christopher's Table night spot. The wine bar proved popular enough that I naturally gravitated to adding a unique, perhaps offbeat, menu. (To this day, I have friends who salivate at the memory of my fried chickpeas.)

Christopher's Table thrived as a wine bar. There was a celebration vibe in the place. Word spread. People arrived from farther and farther away. I was delighted. It felt like *we* had "arrived."

And then came the *Phantom Gourmet*.

I was stunned when the first contact came, from a producer: "We're thinking of doing a segment on Christopher's Table." *Gah! Television!?*

Step 1: The producer pays a visit, all alone, and you just chat. At this point, I think, the producer was really just checking in person to make sure I wasn't a toothless troll. And she needed to be sure that our space wasn't some front for a meth lab. But it was painless enough, we got along, and yeah, okay, this *Phantom Gourmet* episode can happen.

Step 2: You wait. This nearly killed me. Almost six months went by—because the *Phantom*'s scouting operation is always looking way into the future. They don't call you on Sunday and set something up on Monday and then shoot a segment on Tuesday.

Step 3: The producer calls, and you have a heart attack. "We're ready. I have a camera person. Let's pick a date."

I grew up with the *Phantom Gourmet*. Back in the day, it was an honest restaurant review. They could come in and pan you. "Your steak wasn't cooked right. We're giving you two stars. You suck." But then the *Phantom Gourmet* team realized this wasn't a good business plan. They began reviewing only restaurants they *liked*. Result: once you were featured on the *Phantom Gourmet*, you were slammed for months, because the *Phantom* had an amazing following and everyone who saw the segment about your restaurant *had to go check it out!*

All ajitter, I began planning the evening. When the *Phantom Gourmet* is there shooting, you don't want five people scattered across the room in uncomfortable silence. So I assiduously "papered the audience" with friendly faces. The basic pitch was simple: All the food is free; you only pay for alcohol. Eat all night!

You might expect the *Phantom Gourmet* to arrive with a crew of fourteen. But no. The producer showed up at 4:00 p.m. with a camera operator and an assistant. That was it.

We'd closed early for setup. No customers coming and going. The producer had already looked at the menu and worked out with me what they wanted to see. Not to eat. Just to see. It's the great question of our age, I guess: What will look good on camera? "Let's see the chicken potpie." "Let's see the short ribs and polenta." "Nah, no tuna. Won't look good on camera."

Now it's a matter of bringing out the chicken potpie on a plate, looking perfect, and the producer setting it on a table with some staging, a wine glass, a napkin, and . . . "Lights! Camera! Action!" We're shooting a plate of chicken potpie!

Then the producer takes a fork and breaks open the chicken potpie. Camera zooms in!

Dish after dish, they shoot the food.

Actually, the producer did taste some of it. "Talk about the chicken potpie," she said. She took notes.

Then there was an interview with me behind the bar. They previewed the questions they would be asking so I could respond brilliantly. "Give us the sound bites." I wasn't entirely brilliant. "Uh, let's do that again. Didn't sound quite right." "Okay, again, please." (Hey, I could barely admit to being a chef—you want me to be a movie star too!?)

At the appointed hour, ready or not, we had to open the doors to our invited guests. At which point the crew started shooting atmospheric B-roll stuff. The camera moved through the crowded room; narration would be added later by the host, who was never actually there. Happy people filled the bar, more people jammed into couches and tables, filling our little space.

Why was the *Phantom Gourmet* attracted to a tiny wine bar on an obscure street in a small town thirty miles outside Boston?

I think it was our chalkboard.

Oh yeah, I haven't yet mentioned the chalkboard.

On the wall behind the bar, I mounted a huge chalkboard with a simple grid design. This was how we managed our famous Buy a Friend a Drink program.

Here's how it worked: A person *at* Christopher's Table could buy a drink for a friend who was *not* at Christopher's Table. The drink was paid for in advance, and we would reach out to the recipient on social media and alert them that they had a drink waiting for them at Christopher's Table; they could come in and claim it at their convenience.

The chalkboard columns held the information of purchaser, recipient, and beverage of choice.

And when *they* arrived to collect on their gift, they could hardly resist buying a drink for one of their own friends. *Drink it forward!*

The producer took me to the chalkboard and told me that the host of the program wanted to buy the *Phantom* a drink. I dutifully took up a stick of chalk, camera rolling, and wrote the host's first name, then chose a drink, and in the recipient position I wrote *Phantom*.

When the *Phantom Gourmet* broadcast the episode featuring Christopher's Table, they led with the chalkboard, and proceeded to talk about it *a lot*. It was a warm and fuzzy stroke of marketing genius! Kaboom!

I would like to take full credit for the Buy a Friend a Drink strategy, but I can't take any at all. It was all Fridge.

Fridge was, as you can guess, a large person. He had the worst job in the world. He was a chef, but cooking wasn't his job. He served as "expediter" in the kitchen at Ithaki, a popular Mediterranean restaurant around the corner from Christopher's Table. The expediter is the person in the kitchen who bridges that awful breach between the servers, who are dealing with the customers, and the cooks, who are dealing with the food. The expediter looks at the ticket and *organizes* everything—on the fly.

"This table needs calamari."

"This table needs lamb shank."

"This table needs a salad with this but not that."

Whatever was needed, Fridge called it out to the kitchen staff.

"Doug, I need a Caesar. Terry, I need a Greek, no dressing. Vinny,

I need a lamb shank, well done." (Who ruins a lamb shank by cooking it *well done*? Such is the expediter's life. Living with this insanity.)

But it wasn't just this. It was *timing*. Fridge would have to *orchestrate* it all, because he knew you needed the salad first, and how long it would take to make the salad, and he would communicate with the server how and when to take it to the table, and . . .

You know how frustrating it is, sitting in a restaurant, when your salad arrives late and your entrée arrives early and you have all these plates of food in front of you, and you're feeling somewhat foolish? You've just experienced an expediter failure.

Yeah, wow. Complicated job. Awful, awful job. Horrible pressure. Unfuckingbelievable stress. On those few occasions in my restaurant career when someone mentioned to me the possibility of taking a job as expediter, I absolutely froze in fear. I'd rather stick a fork in my eye. But Fridge and I developed a beautiful friendship. I would say, a brotherly relationship. Here's how it began.

Petros, the owner of Ithaki, was an acquaintance of mine. And I also knew most of the people who worked at Ithaki: bartenders, cooks, servers. So when Christopher's Table became a wine bar—only about thirty seconds away from Ithaki—Christopher's Table became the place to go after work for the Ithaki crew.

But these were restaurant people.

So I could meet Ipswich regulars at a table or at the bar at 7:00 p.m., serve various fine upstanding ordinary folk throughout the evening, and everyone would nosh and have a very civilized time.

But by 11:00 p.m., they arrived en masse.

Hordes of battle-weary soldiers began straggling in from Ithaki down the street.

They had spent the entire evening dealing with masses of customers, in a large restaurant, and now they needed to decompress.

Of course, financially, it was great. A room full of industry people, all big drinkers, and for the most part, friends. It was an after-hours party every night.

Fridge was one of these revelers.

He was larger than life. He was the big fat guy! Huge, tall. And nobody you'd want on your bad side.

My love for Fridge is deeply rooted in the fact that I never had to actually work with him. In fact, I would say I maintained something of a "little brother" relationship with him.

I saw Fridge in action. When he was behind the counter, if you weren't doing your job, you were dead. You could be the owner's wife, he didn't care. "You fucking idiot! What the fuck is wrong with you? Get this fucking food out to the dining room!"

But when the evening shift was over, if you'd been in Fridge's line of fire, he'd wrap his arms around you and carry you across the street to Christopher's Table. He would plop you down at our bar, and you wouldn't pay for a drink all night long. *What happens during dinner service . . .* "Yes, I beat the crap out of you during dinner service. And yes, I may beat the crap out of you again tomorrow during dinner service. But for now, it's all good." (I could always tell which of my late-night guests had messed up at Ithaki: Fridge was buying their drinks.)

Fridge was beautiful.

And in the swirl of our friendship, night by day, week by month, I found him in my face, with a curious message: "I saw this somewhere, in a bar. You should try it."

When you own a bar, everyone says, "What you should do is . . ." You learn to shrug it off.

But when Fridge said it, it was different. This was a restaurant person. An industry person. Someone I respected. Someone who could bring you an outlandish idea and you would actually give it a second thought.

So when Fridge explained the Buy a Friend a Drink concept to me, I tried it. I wish I could tell you it was all my idea. But no.

Whenever Fridge visited Christopher's Table and saw the big chalkboard filled with names and drink orders, he was effusive. "You're killing it!" I always reminded him it was his idea, not mine. I loved it.

After a long night of drinking at my place, the Ithaki folks would have to show up at their own place the next day, at 10:00 a.m., to begin prepping. Work hard, play hard, pay the price. Dedicated soldiers, in a weird F'd-up army.

But Fridge, understanding all this, responded with compassion. He would go in early and make gyros. Not the traditional gyros that one might expect from the classical Greek Ithaki menu. These were something you might call "breakfast gyros." Soft, warm pita, loaded with tirokafteri (spicy Greek feta cheese dip); an egg, over easy; tomatoes; onions. One of the most decadent, delicious breakfasts I've ever experienced.

And if you were hung over, it was like heaven.

I wasn't an Ithaki staffer, so the only way I know about this divine gift is because Fridge always sent someone knocking at my door "the morning after."

Fridge would choose the hunkiest man on the Ithaki staff and send him to my kitchen door with a magical gift. A breakfast gyro.

But Fridge was also, entirely, a boots-on-the-ground, grind-it-out, everyday restaurateur. I need dried oregano; can you help me? *Yes, send a busser.* Coffee filters! *Yes, send someone to get them.*

I did the same thing. *I'm out of sugar!* I could run to my back door and find Fridge's staffer with a ten-pound bag.

Fridge became part and parcel of Christopher's Table.

When you arrived at the bar, you were served potato sticks—salty, crunchy bar snacks—before you even ordered a drink. I confess, it was a pain, because at the end of the evening, there were potato sticks all over the floor that needed to be cleaned up. But one night, the potato sticks followed Fridge home.

It was 2:00 a.m. or so. I was home, getting ready for bed, taking off my pants. Something fluttered. I looked down, and dollar bills were floating to the floor. Hilarious. Another night of dancing and debauchery at Christopher's Table.

In my amusement, I had to text Fridge. *Dude! I just took my pants off and all these dollar bills fell out!*

Fridge's response was not what I expected.

F— you. I just took off my pants, and all that fell out were potato sticks.

There were definitely nights where things at Christopher's Table could get a little out of hand, the debauchery was infectious and had us all wanting more . . . even if what we really needed was less.

BUY SOMEONE A DRINK

Spiced Fried Chickpeas

When Christopher's Table transformed from a bakery and prepared-food shop into a wine bar and restaurant, the pace in our kitchen had to change. We were now cooking food to order instead of simply filling our display cases. I remember working with one of our chefs, Joe, to come up with easily executable small plates to serve at the bar. These deliciously spiced chickpeas fit the bill perfectly.

1 (15½-ounce) can chickpeas, rinsed, drained, and patted dry
2 tablespoons cornstarch
¼ cup extra-virgin olive oil
1 teaspoon ground cumin
1 teaspoon smoked paprika
¼ teaspoon white sugar
½ teaspoon kosher salt
¼ teaspoon pepper

Makes 6–8 snack servings

In a medium bowl, toss the chickpeas with the cornstarch. Transfer them to a fine-mesh strainer and shake to remove the excess cornstarch.

In a 10-inch skillet over medium-high heat, heat the oil until shimmering. Add the chickpeas and cook, stirring occasionally, until golden brown and crisp, about 5 minutes.

Remove from the heat and stir in the cumin, paprika, sugar, salt, and pepper. Toss to coat and serve warm.

Roasted Red Pepper and Goat Cheese Arancini

What to do with leftover risotto? Make arancini! We served these delicious morsels with a roasted-tomato dipping sauce at the bar at Christopher's Table. A light-bodied pinot grigio with hints of fruit complements the savory elements of the arancini.

3 cups low-sodium chicken broth
¼ teaspoon kosher salt
1 cup arborio rice
½ cup jarred roasted red peppers, diced small
2 large eggs
½ cup grated Parmesan cheese
1½ cups breadcrumbs, divided
4 ounces goat cheese
2 tablespoons chopped fresh parsley
Vegetable oil, for frying

24–36 pieces

Bring the broth and salt to a boil in a medium saucepan over medium-high heat. Stir in the rice. Reduce the heat to low and simmer until tender, about 20 minutes.

Fold in the roasted red peppers. Spread the mixture on a parchment-lined baking sheet and let it cool completely.

Beat the eggs in a large bowl, then stir in the cooled rice, Parmesan, and ⅔ cup of the breadcrumbs. Shape the mixture into 16 (1½-inch) balls.

Combine the goat cheese and parsley in a bowl. Pressing your finger into the center of each rice ball, insert 2 teaspoons of the goat cheese mixture, then pinch the rice around the filling to enclose it.

Put the remaining breadcrumbs in a shallow bowl. Roll the balls in the breadcrumbs and place them on a parchment-lined baking sheet.

Loosely cover and refrigerate for 1 to 6 hours. (If refrigerating for more than an hour, roll in additional breadcrumbs before frying.)

Heat ½ inch of vegetable oil in a large saucepan over medium heat until a deep-fry thermometer registers 350°F. Working in batches, fry rice balls, turning until golden brown on all sides, about 4 minutes. Remove with a slotted spoon and drain on paper towels. Season with salt and serve.

Individual Chicken Potpies

I don't often boast about the food that I make, but I have been known to puff up my chest and throw down when it comes to my chicken potpie. At Christopher's Table we served these in individual crocks with a side of buttery mashed potatoes.

Filling:

5 to 6 boneless chicken breasts, cut into 1-inch pieces
3 tablespoons olive oil
5 cups chicken stock
2 chicken bouillon cubes
12 tablespoons unsalted butter
2 yellow onions, chopped (2 cups)
¾ cup all-purpose flour
2 teaspoons kosher salt
½ teaspoon pepper
¼ cup heavy cream
4 carrots, cut into half circles and blanched for 2 minutes (2 cups)
1 (10-ounce) package frozen peas
1½ cups frozen small pearl onions
½ cup minced fresh parsley

Crust:

2 cups all-purpose flour
1 tablespoon baking powder
1 teaspoon kosher salt
1 teaspoon sugar
¼ pound (1 stick) cold unsalted butter, diced
¾ cup half-and-half
½ cup chopped fresh parsley
1 egg mixed with 1 tablespoon water, for egg wash

Makes 6-8 servings

Preheat the oven to 375°F.

Toss the cut-up chicken with the olive oil and place it on a sheet pan. Sprinkle generously with salt and pepper. Roast for 30 to 35 minutes, or until cooked through.

In a small saucepan, heat the chicken stock and dissolve the bouillon cubes in it.

In a large pot, melt the butter and sauté the onions over medium-low heat for 10 to 15 minutes, until translucent. Add the flour to make a roux and cook over low heat, stirring constantly, for 2 minutes. Add the hot chicken stock to the roux. Simmer over low heat for 1 more minute, stirring, until thick. Add the salt, pepper, and heavy cream.

Mix in the cubed chicken, carrots, peas, pearl onions, and parsley.

Place the filling in individual ovenproof ramekins. Put the ramekins on a sheet pan lined with parchment or wax paper.

To make the crust, combine the flour, baking powder, salt, and sugar in an electric mixer fitted with a paddle attachment. Add the butter and mix on low speed until the butter is pea size. Add the half-and-half and combine on low speed. Mix in the parsley.

Dump the dough out on a well-floured board and roll it out to less than ½ inch thick. Cut out circles that are slightly larger than the ramekins (I use a large round cookie cutter).

Arrange the dough circles on top of the filling. Crimp and trim the excess overhang. Brush with the egg wash, and place the sheet pan with the ramekins in the oven. Bake for 30 minutes, or until the crusts are brown and the filling is bubbly.

175

RECIPE: INDIVIDUAL CHICKEN POTPIES

Spicy Thai Steamed Mussels in Coconut Curry Broth

I was lucky enough to be invited to cook with a local chef while I was traveling through Southeast Asia. We cooked in her tiny kitchen and produced a wide variety of Asian specialties. My favorite was her coconut curry broth. Once we put these mussels on the menu at Christopher's Table, we never took them off.

5 pounds mussels (preferably cultivated)
3 limes
1 (13½-ounce) can unsweetened coconut milk
⅓ cup dry white wine
1½ tablespoons Thai red curry paste
1½ tablespoons minced garlic
1 tablespoon fish sauce
1 tablespoon sugar
2 cups fresh cilantro sprigs
Lime wedges and crusty bread, for serving

Makes 4–6 servings

Scrub the mussels well and remove the beards.

Squeeze enough juice from the limes to measure ⅓ cup.

In an 8-quart pot, boil the lime juice, coconut milk, wine, curry paste, garlic, fish sauce, and sugar over high heat, stirring, for 2 minutes. Add the mussels, tossing to combine.

Cook the mussels, covered, stirring occasionally, until opened, 7 to 8 minutes. Discard any unopened mussels. Chop the cilantro and toss with the mussels.

Serve with lime wedges and crusty bread. Trust me, you are going to want to mop up that delicious broth!

Red Wine–Braised Short Ribs with Creamy Polenta

Obviously, at a wine bar, we cooked with a lot of wine. These short ribs braise for hours in a hearty full-bodied red—making them a perfect cold-weather comfort dish.

Short ribs:
- 3 pounds boneless beef short ribs, about 6 pieces
- 2 cups full-bodied dry red wine (such as côtes du rhône or malbec), divided
- 1 cup beef broth
- 1 head garlic, sliced in half horizontally and papery outer layers removed
- 3 to 4 fresh rosemary or thyme sprigs, or 2 teaspoons herbes de Provence

Polenta:
- 1 cup milk
- 2 cups chicken broth
- 2 teaspoons kosher salt
- ½ cup cornmeal
- 3 tablespoons butter
- ⅓ cup grated Parmesan cheese

Makes 6–8 servings

Preheat the oven to 475°F.

Put the ribs on a large rimmed baking sheet. Sprinkle the meat liberally on all sides with salt and pepper.

Roast the ribs for 20 minutes, until sizzling and forming a brown crust. Transfer the ribs to a roasting pan or baking dish large enough to hold them in one layer. Turn the oven down to 275°F.

Pour ½ cup of the wine onto the baking sheet and scrape up any brown bits, then pour it all over the ribs. Add in the remaining 1½ cups wine and beef broth. Toss in the garlic and herb sprigs.

Cover the pan tightly with foil and return it to the oven for 3½ hours, or until the meat is very tender and breaks apart with a fork. Remove from the oven and let the meat rest, covered, for 20 minutes.

Shred the meat with a fork and pour over the pan juices to keep it moist (skim the fat if you like).

To make the polenta, bring the milk and chicken broth to a boil in a heavy 2- or 3-quart pot. Stir in the salt, then slowly stir in the cornmeal a little at a time to avoid lumps.

Turn the heat down to low and cook, stirring frequently, until the polenta thickens, about 25 minutes. Stir in the butter and cheese. Cover and keep warm until serving.

Red Wine–Poached Pears with Mascarpone Filling

The wine bar at Christopher's Table was dark and intimate, with its red damask walls, cozy couches, and chandeliers. These sexy poached pears fit right in and were the perfect ending to your night with us.

6 firm Bartlett pears
1 bottle red wine
1 cup pomegranate juice
3 cups water
1 vanilla bean, whole
2 cinnamon sticks
2 bay leaves
2 cups sugar
2 (8-ounce) containers mascarpone cheese, softened
½ cup heavy cream
Pinch of ground cinnamon
½ cup powdered sugar
2 tablespoons butter
10 to 15 crushed gingersnaps

Makes 6 servings

Peel the pears but leave the stem intact.

In a large saucepan, bring the wine, pomegranate juice, and cold water to a simmer. Split the vanilla bean lengthwise and add it to the wine mixture. Add the cinnamon sticks, bay leaves, and sugar. Add the pears to the liquid and simmer about 20 minutes, or until tender.

Cool the pears in the wine mixture to room temperature. (You can refrigerate them in the poaching liquid until you're ready to fill them.)

Remove the stems from the pears and set the stems aside. Core the pears with an apple corer, leaving the pear whole.

Whisk together the mascarpone cheese, heavy cream, ground cinnamon, and powdered sugar until smooth. Transfer the mixture to a pastry bag. Pipe the filling into the cored pears and finish by putting the stems gently into the mascarpone filling on top.

Bring the sauce to a simmer and reduce by half. Add the butter to the reduced sauce and stir until combined. Spoon generously over the pears. Cool to room temperature before serving. Dust the finished pears with the crushed gingersnaps.

PART VIII

DEBAUCHERY BY DEGREES

Where's Daddy?

There are levels of debauchery.

At level 1, there's just drinking and yelling and being funny, and waking up with potato sticks falling out of your pants.

At level 2, there's a beer and wine license, so you have to close up by a certain hour, after which you can't legally sell alcohol. But... If you're giving it away, does that really count?

Christopher's Table had two enormous storefront windows. A number of friends, perhaps a dozen, were reveling. Two in the morning—unheard of in Ipswich, Massachusetts.

Bright lights suddenly shot through the front windows.

High beams. A cop was parked across the street, in the parking lot at the bank.

The cop was sending a message. *I see you. I know what you're doing in there.*

My brilliant response: "Nobody move!"

It didn't work. The cop car's high beams didn't move either.

My phone rang.

"Hello, this is the Ipswich police department. We have an officer calling in, saying there are people in your place of business..."

Yes, sorry. Level 2 debauchery.

Then maybe sometimes there were some VIPs at Christopher's Table, and at closing time, as the beloved regulars wandered out, the place would close down and the lights would go out and—yes, we learned our level 2 lesson—we would move back into the kitchen area. You couldn't be seen from the street if you were in the kitchen. The only light was from the hood over the twelve-burner stove. And the hood fan, over the stove, sucked out all the smoke. Which was important, back then, when weed was illegal. And weed was everywhere. People sat on the counters and talked and laughed and smoked and . . . other stuff. Not a lot of people. Just a few. Just once in a while.

I didn't set out to make it such a place. I liked to think that the place itself had such a destiny. I'd heard plenty of stories about what went on in this building generations ago: pool tables in the basement, drunks spending the night, homeless people sleeping on the floor, a big fire. Maybe there was an Amityville not-quite-horror type of thing going on here. Maybe (I told myself) the debauchery wasn't really my fault!

One night, I was entertaining a few friends along with a few of their friends who were not known to me. As a joint was being passed from person to person, a certain person felt compelled to decline the offer, and tell the truth, the whole truth, and nothing but the truth.

"I'm a police officer."

Gulp.

Fortunately, this was not an Ipswich police officer.

"So I can't, uh, partake."

As I secretly, silently, freaked out, I offered a brilliant response: "Want a whoopie pie?"

He did.

We're still friends.

Don't tell me you can't bribe an officer of the law. In my experience, you say, "Want a whoopie pie?" and you get away with everything.

Food brought all kinds of people together. Not everyone at Christopher's Table was a weed-smoking, late-night, whoopie-pie-eating animal; some of them were simply normal, straightlaced folks. As part of the process of converting the store into a wine bar, we needed a speaker system in the ceiling so we could provide ambient music. I hired a company to install the system. A super nice guy named James showed up to do the work. He was straight and straightlaced—he also happened to be really cute! As his work climbing up and down ladders into the ceiling took him into the lunch hour, I made him a chicken salad sandwich.

And he fell in love. With my chicken salad. Made with my mom's recipe. A staple from the very first days of Christopher's Table.

Long after the sound system installation had been completed, cute James was still regularly returning to Christopher's Table for the chicken salad. We became friends, and he became something of a fixture. People actually took to calling him Cute James.

Cute James was single, so he liked hanging out at the bar and staying late. He didn't smoke, he barely ever drank—hard cider was about as far as he would go—but more than once he found himself surrounded by revelers of a distinctly different stripe. Cute James was a hit with the ladies, but he just kept to himself, minding his own business. At the first sign of trouble, James was a fiercely loyal and protective pal.

One late night in the kitchen, with some serious level 3 debauchery underway in the light of the hood lamp, I saw another light cutting into the darkness. It was coming from the open fridge.

"Don't mind me," Cute James said innocently. He was laying hold of his own drug of choice. Chicken salad.

It was the best of times. It was the worst of times.

It was the heyday of Christopher's Table. Profits and spirits ran high. Our wine bar golden era.

But I began to realize . . . it was not what I signed up for.

This was not the lifestyle of choice for the parent of two small children.

I had signed up to be the guy who wakes up early and makes coffee, cupcakes, and whoopie pies. Now I had dollar bills and potato sticks falling out of my pants and someone's T-shirt under the garde-manger station. I loved every minute of it. Fun, crazy, reckless times. But not sustainable. Bob was supportive of my entrepreneurship, but I could tell that the late nights and time away from my family were wearing thin. With Bob's help, I realized this was not what I had set out to do. To be. I could look into the future and see something sad. I could see a divorce. I could see my children struggling.

Yes, the business itself was sustainable, even though it was never going to be a massive moneymaker—because size matters. You need a certain number of tables, of seats. How many times a night can you turn those two-tops? Christopher's Table could only ever be the size that it was, could only make so much of an impact. There was a "ceiling" to our profitability.

Maybe I could convert that space in the back? Expand our serving area? Generate more revenue? No, the investment required would make my husband's head explode.

To my shame, I put Bob through more arguments than I can count. In matters of money he always won. I'm Italian—emotional, irrational. He's a cerebral warrior.

"When we met," he said, rationally, "we talked a lot about what we wanted in life."

True.

"You wanted to own a house with a yard, and have a dog . . ."

Also true.

"But I don't remember you ever saying you wanted to own a bar."

Bob was right. This wasn't my dream. I had more or less just fallen into it. Mr. Muffin Man had somehow gotten lost and stumbled his way into the kitchen at 2:00 a.m. at debauchery level 3. This had never been on my radar screen. This had just happened. Success, like shit, happens.

"I do remember," Bob went on, "you said you wanted to be a dad."

Truly, truly true. I urgently, fully, totally wanted to be a dad.

Our son Alex was ten. Our son Lucas was six. For most of the Christopher's Table years, with Bob working at a hospital and me running the shop, we'd had to employ a nanny. In the early years, I left the house so early, to make my bread and my cookies and my croissants, I couldn't take the boys to school. In the wine bar years, I started later—I could do school drop-off duty—but I worked till the wee hours of the morning more often than not, missing dinners and bedtime. Either way, the same total number of hours, just a different chunk of the clock.

So at the end of each school day, it was Nikia, our amazing nanny, who picked the boys up, either at the school or the bus stop. At dinnertime, she brought the boys to Christopher's Table to pick up dinner; then the three of them went home to eat it. Until finally Bob got home from work, and Nikia would depart.

Nikia was wonderful—a hardworking single mom, putting herself through school, trying to build a life for herself and her young son. But for my boys, she was still a nanny. She wasn't the dad I wanted to be.

Sometimes, you have to say, "Ya know what? This success—it ain't success."

No regrets. Loved the laughter, loved the stories and the spotlight. But at the end of the day, it wasn't who I wanted to be, and needed to be, as a parent and a partner.

Bob and I went to the boys' school for an open house. Each child's artwork had been assembled in a binder for the parents to peruse. I opened Lucas's binder . . .

There's Lucas and his dog.
There's Lucas with his dad Bob and their dog.
There's Lucas and his brother.
There's Lucas and his brother and his dad Bob.
There's Lucas playing hockey, with his dad Bob watching.
There's Lucas with his dad Bob.
Page by page, my heart sank deeper.

I'm an asshole, I said to myself. *I'm nowhere to be found in Lucas's life.* Where was I when all this happened? I finally made an appearance, in one picture, on one of the final pages. I was at work, making cupcakes.

At that moment, the scales began to tip. Christopher's Table didn't feel so much like success anymore. It had all come at a serious cost.

Sometime later, Bob and I were on vacation in Bar Harbor, Maine. I turned to him. "When we get back," I said, "I'm going to close the shop."

Bob's response was perfectly appropriate to the moment, perfectly loving. He didn't rerun my errors in judgment. He didn't restate the wisdom of his previous arguments. He just said one gentle, completely beautiful word.

"Okay."

People talk.

When a business closes, everyone tends to form their own opinions and spout their own assumptions.

Christopher wasn't making enough money.

Christopher didn't make the right moves.

Christopher was exhausted.

Christopher didn't try hard enough.

All conjecture, and all wrong.

There was a part of me that felt guilty about letting people down, the people who loved Christopher's Table. I had been embraced by the Ipswich community. Against all odds, they had accepted and welcomed the wonderful craziness of Christopher's Table. I felt deeply conflicted about closing the door on my customers, friends, and staunch supporters. It was always about people, food was just a connection to the community—and now I was closing off that connection. You can know you're doing the right thing and it can still be hard. And I didn't like anyone assuming the decision was anything more than what it really was. I was choosing my family. I was packing up my muffin tins and I was going *home*.

I came away feeling that I had the best reason ever for closing my business. Not for lack of money. Not for lack of trying. Not for inferior cupcakes.

I closed Christopher's Table because it had taken on a life of its own, and it wasn't the life I had dedicated myself to.

People dropped in, after the doleful closure announcement, to pay their last respects. Eventually, after all the bittersweet goodbyes, there was one final farewell extravaganza—I think there's a photo of me dancing on the bar with a couple of friends.

And then . . . *fade to black*.

My sons entered a new season of life: "We'll see Daddy more. He'll cook dinner for us at home instead of the shop." I liked that.

I sold my knives, sold my equipment. Sold that beloved table—to someone who promised to also love it very much.

I made a self-indulgent video, set to dramatic music, a photo retrospective of Christopher's Table highlights from over the years, and sent it out to my mailing list. It was a cathartic exercise, I guess. But it wasn't enough. Eventually, I came around to a new idea for connecting, a new way of using food to reach out to people: *I think I'll write a book!*

And here I am.

It was never about cupcakes, or Paris, or drag queens, or dinner on a farm. It wasn't about a business model or a bottom line. For me, it was and still is about the power of food bringing people together.

And here we are. Together.

See how food works?

ABOUT THE AUTHOR

Christopher J. DeStefano is an award-winning chef, entrepreneur, and food writer who has been cooking professionally since 2006. In 2008, DeStefano opened Christopher's Table, his celebrated prepared-food shop and restaurant on the North Shore of Boston. He has written food articles for local publications, led culinary tours through Paris, and hosted hundreds of guests at elaborate dinners in bucolic farm fields as part of his widely acclaimed Dinner on the Farm series.

In 2014, after closing Christopher's Table, DeStefano managed some of the Boston area's top restaurants, including OAK Long Bar + Kitchen in the venerable Fairmont Copley Plaza. In 2019, DeStefano created an online culinary brand, Table Manners (www.tablemanners.shop), which sells homemade baked goods, freshly prepared foods, and unique culinary gifts. In 2022, Table Manners was recognized by *Northshore* magazine as the area's best personal-chef service.

www.ingramcontent.com/pod-product-compliance
Lightning Source LLC
Chambersburg PA
CBHW061406010526
44119CB00011B/279